T0278773

Waving
Goodbye

Waving Goodbye

Life After Loss

Warren Kozak

A POST HILL PRESS BOOK
ISBN: 979-8-88845-338-4
ISBN (eBook): 979-8-88845-339-1

Waving Goodbye:
Life After Loss
© 2024 by Warren Kozak
All Rights Reserved

Post Hill Press
New York • Nashville
posthillpress.com

Published in the United States of America
2 3 4 5 6 7 8 9 10

One last time ...
For Lisa and Claire

"Had the story come full circle in the way that stories end, they would have walked quietly, Catherine and Harry, into the rest of their life, knowing that in the end the whole world is nothing more than what you remember and what you love …."

In Sunlight and in Shadow, Mark Helprin

TABLE OF CONTENTS

PROLOGUE

WHEN I WAS FIVE YEARS old, an unusually large number of women around my parents—all in their 30s—died of cancer in a short span of time: my father's sister (my aunt Anita), my mother's best friend (Mrs. Arensky), the other Girl Scout troop leader with my mom (Mrs. DeWitt), and our next-door neighbor (Mrs. Wickesberg).

Years later, I asked my mother what that time was like for her.

"It felt like a lottery," she said, as her entire expression darkened; she seemed lost in memory.

Before I was enrolled in school and when my older sisters were already there, I was home alone with my mother during the day. Sometimes Mrs. Wickesberg came over from next door after the older kids were off to school. They would sit at the kitchen table, have coffee together, and chat. It was, in many ways, a very typical 1950s neighborhood.

When all the bad events began to unfold, nothing was explained to us, but children, even five-year-olds, hear conversations, they pick up on everything, especially things that don't fit.

I used to play next door with her daughter, Gail, and I remember being in the living room one day while Mrs.

Wickesberg was lying down on the couch. I knew something wasn't right. She was always busy in the kitchen or directing us in some way. Besides, mothers didn't lie on the couch in the middle of the day.

Sometime later, it must have been a couple of years later because I knew how to read by then, I was over at their house when I happened to walk past a closet just as Gail's father opened the door. I glanced up and saw a box on the shelf labeled: "Kay's Childhood." Looking back, I think I immediately understood what it was because it saddened me and it has stayed with me all these years.

One day in that first year, I ran out of paper towels and went into our storage room to get another roll. Glancing up, I froze in place.

There on the top shelf, I saw the box I put together several months earlier that I unwittingly labeled: "Lisa's Childhood."

I just stood there and thought:

My God, I've become Mr. Wickesberg.

CHAPTER 1

New Year's Day

AT 4:30 AM ON JANUARY 1, 2018, my wife took her final breath and was pronounced dead.

Over the previous four years, Lisa's heart had been structurally destroyed by amyloidosis ("Imagine sand coursing through your bloodstream," one of her doctors told me). This disease was an offshoot of a primary illness, a rare blood cancer with a ridiculously long name, Waldenstrom Macroglobulinemia.

I was standing over Lisa, and at the moment her heart stopped, I suddenly had trouble breathing. Even though I had anticipated this event for at least two years, even though I was given a pretty accurate description of what would unfold in her final days, and even though I imagined I would be calm and even heroic when it finally happened, I was, instead, completely dumbfounded. Shocked. I was gulping for air and I found it hard to think straight.

I was as far from heroic as one could imagine.

At the immediate moment of a death, Catholics cross themselves. Protestants may recite the Lord's Prayer or the

23rd Psalm. I am Jewish and there is a very short Hebrew prayer that Jews are supposed to say out loud at this transitional moment. "Baruch Dayan Ha Emet." "Blessed is He, the true Judge." Simple, to the point, I even had the prayer book opened nearby in anticipation. Yet, as hard as I tried, I could not read it. I struggled, but my brain simply wouldn't function and the words I saw on the page would not come out of my mouth. This had never happened to me before. I really mangled it and then just gave up entirely.

With enormous effort, I settled myself down to the point that I could breathe normally again, probably because I was suddenly faced with a multitude of new tasks, the first of which I dreaded most. I went into our daughter's room, woke Claire up, and told her it was all over, her mother had just died.

From the moment we found out Lisa was pregnant 20 years earlier, I felt an immediate sense of protection for this embryo, the likes of which I had never felt before. That feeling never dissipated. Now, 20 years later, I could do nothing to protect my child from the greatest hurt of her life.

I stayed in Claire's room for a long time hugging her as she cried. Then I brought her into our bedroom, where I held her over the bed, crying.

Finally, I called the funeral home and waited for them to come and take Lisa away from us forever.

CHAPTER 2

Past, Present, and Future Time

As a child, I was fascinated by the large digital clock at the Cape Canaveral launch pad for the early Mercury flights. Everyone focused on the countdown, but most people didn't realize that as soon as it reached zero and the Redstone rocket lifted off with the astronaut onboard, the big clock immediately counted in the other direction: :01, :02, :03… so there was a record of the elapsed time of the entire mission.

Throughout her illness, I saw Lisa's cancer and the end of her life as a sort of countdown to her moment of death. But, as soon as she exhaled her last breath, the clock didn't stop. Like the NASA clock, it kept moving in the other direction, recording the continuum of a new time, the time *after* Lisa. That clock would just keep ticking, and this would be my new reality.

There is something else. It was almost as if a toggle-switch had been abruptly flipped on me. For four years,

I was completely engrossed in helping someone with a serious illness. Now, I was suddenly forced to contend with that same person who had moved into a completely different realm, a mysterious realm filled with unknowns.

As I entered this new phase of my life, I faced a myriad of new decisions that just kept piling up one after the other. The first: I was torn between not letting Lisa make the trip to the funeral home alone with strangers or staying with our daughter. I rarely left Lisa's side during her illness and this commitment didn't fade after she died.

When Claire insisted she would be alright by herself, I helped the two men lift Lisa and put her on a gurney. I became very upset when her head fell violently backward, and I rushed over to cradle and support it, unable to believe, incapable of believing, that, of course, it didn't matter anymore. She wouldn't feel this or anything else.

She was placed in a body bag that one of the attendants zipped up and, once again, although the rational part of me knew she wasn't breathing anymore, the irrational part worried that there would be no air inside for her. Add to those two disconnected concerns, there was one more big one–I worried that she wasn't really dead, that a mistake had been made, and she would wake up in the body bag, or in the funeral home, terrified.

I was desperately trying to think rationally, but these aberrant thoughts kept intruding. The obvious reason–I could not accept the fact that my wife, this woman I loved so much, was really dead.

The men were understanding and let me ride along with them the short distance to the funeral home, about 20 blocks. I remember absolutely nothing about the trip. Lisa was taken to a cold storage room, which I found ironic, since it was much colder outside. I sat with the funeral director who was kind, patient, and efficient. He helped me make all the arrangements including choosing a casket (I asked for a plain pine box). We worked out the transportation that would be necessary to fly Lisa to Wisconsin for burial. I handed him a credit card like I was buying a cup of coffee … and then just got up, said goodbye, and walked back home.

It was still early on New Year's Day and most people were in bed. You could see the remnants of last night's revelries all over the sidewalks. While people had been celebrating in the streets and at parties, my little family had been devastated with our greatest catastrophe.

All the way back home, I couldn't shake Lisa's color when I last saw her. She always had very pure, light skin ("White girl!" She jokingly called herself), but her color quickly changed to an alabaster white, almost translucent, like I had never seen before. I also remember thinking she still looked so beautiful.

And now another strong feeling of guilt: I felt terrible leaving her there. Lisa lost her own mother when she was 12 years old. Death and its formal representative, the funeral home, made her very uncomfortable. I had been by her side throughout her entire illness. Now, I just left her in a place she hated and feared, and I just walked away.

CHAPTER 3

Storm Warnings

THROUGHOUT THAT FIRST DAY, OUTWARDLY I appeared to be normal, performing the rituals that force us to remain in the world of the living: notifying family and friends, coordinating travel plans for the burial, writing the obit for the *New York Times*. Claire and I picked out a photo we both loved for the paper. Later, we composed a mass email telling everyone what had happened while they were asleep and giving them the details of the services. Email: the new telegraphy for the saddest news.

All of this was made more difficult because we had to race to transport Lisa's body from New York City (where we lived) to Wisconsin (where I grew up) and get ourselves out there and back before an impending snowstorm cancelled all air traffic.

Claire and I flew to Milwaukee and met Lisa's brother and his wife, who flew from San Francisco. The four of us spent the night with my closest friends. I remember how warm and cheerful their home was, filled with light, with all their beautiful Christmas decorations still up. What would have been a dark night in the middle of a Wisconsin winter was made infinitely brighter by their kindness and caring. Amazingly, their large golden retriever, George, seemed to understand what had happened and attached himself to Claire, sleeping with her on her bed and giving her great comfort.

The next morning, we held the short burial service at the graveside in a howling wind and -5° temperature. Lisa absolutely hated the cold, and standing there, with each strong gust of wind, I thought that when my time comes and I am lowered right next to her, her first question will be: "What the hell were you thinking??? It is so damned cold here!!"

One more item on the long list of things I will have to answer for.

I thought it would be just us, the rabbi, and family members, but all of our neighbors from our lake house were waiting outside in the freezing cold, along with high school friends I hadn't seen in 40 years, and others. My college roommate and his wife had driven up from Chicago. When they came up to me, I thought: *What nice people to come for this, I wonder who they are?* I had no idea at first because their heads were completely wrapped in hats and scarves.

In the hardest hour of our lives, the presence of each person there touched us deeply and supported us. It still touches me to this day. It would have been so upsetting being there all by ourselves. Instead, we were surrounded by family and friends and kindness.

The Jewish burial ceremony is mercifully short, which was especially appreciated on this day with the gusts of wind and biting cold. I spoke briefly, mainly thanking everyone for being there and trying desperately to say something about Lisa that might capture her. I would work on a eulogy for the larger memorial service planned for New York at the end of the week. The rabbi, whom we did not know, but who was a friend of my cousin, spoke beautifully and was comforting. The Hebrew prayers were recited, the casket was lowered into the ground, and we each symbolically placed a shovelful of dirt over it–again, a Jewish tradition to "assist" in the burial.

I stood there over the open grave, looking down, holding Claire. We held each other. I wish I could write what my feelings were at that seminal moment in our lives. I cannot. I was completely overwhelmed with a multitude of thoughts. My chief concern for Claire overrode my feelings for Lisa. We just stood there looking down at the casket, bracing ourselves against the wind, and for the first time in my life, I understood why people have been known to jump into the grave. It almost seemed like a natural thing to do. Claire later told me she was thinking the same thing, holding herself back. We held each other. It was just impossible to comprehend that after everything we had been through together, we would now just leave her there.

And we did.

We went directly back to the airport from the cemetery and were lucky to get on one of the last flights out before most air traffic was shut down due to the approaching storm.

As the plane took off and I looked down at the icy white landscape, the last wave of guilt came over me, leaving Lisa in that frozen field all alone.

CHAPTER 4

The Shiva

UPON OUR RETURN TO NEW YORK, there was the one week of public visits to our home. In Judaism, it's called Shiva[1], but practically all religions and cultures have some variant on this theme.

In the final scene of *To Kill a Mockingbird*, Scout explains the ways Americans in the South respond: "Neighbors bring food for death, flowers for sickness, and little things in between."

We would soon experience all three.

For seven days, people just kept coming through the front door—friends, family, work colleagues, neighbors, the guys from the locker room at the gym, my synagogue buddies from the morning minyan, teachers and parents from Claire's school, her former classmates, Lisa's work colleagues and some of her patients, along with grade

---

1   The literal meaning of Shiva in Hebrew is *seven*, for the seven days of
     this period of mourning.

school, high school and college friends who came from Philadelphia, where she grew up.

People you want to see. People you *don't* want to see. All of which forces you to maintain a social front.

The Shiva's purpose is for the community to support the bereaved during this incredibly hard time, and it works. Seeing these people confirmed to me that Lisa was important to others as well, and although I knew this on one level, I needed it reinforced right now. Seeing everyone certainly made me feel less alone. But I believe the most important purpose of the Shiva is this: it forces us to go through the motions of being human. It forces us to relearn how to talk again, how to walk again. It forces us to take those first steps back into life.

In many ways, I felt like I was acting through those days. I was playing the role of *Normal Me*, which I wasn't at all. It would be a long time before I would be *Normal Me* again.

I also knew that if left on my own, I would have been completely lost, desolate, dead. It doesn't surprise me that widowers die at a higher rate soon after they lose their wives of many years. Our equilibrium is thrown off in the most astounding way one could ever imagine, and this new stress is all consuming. I was healthy and relatively young, so I survived.

The shiva has very prescribed guidelines, giving one a sense of structure, when we don't even realize that some sort of structure, some regularity and, especially, some guidance is desperately needed at this moment. People can't think rationally for themselves. That's because every guidepost in your life has been suddenly upended in the most dramatic way.[2]

The weeklong ritual is really quite brilliant, and even though I had gone through Shivas for grandparents and both parents, this was the first time I truly grasped its wisdom and absolute necessity.

Two years later, when COVID shut down the world, I felt worse not for the victims, but for their survivors who could not have normal funerals and Shivas or wakes. If Claire and I had to come back from the burial all alone, that would have been the loneliest time imaginable. It was that one week of visits that kept me going during the worst seven days of my life.

Throughout it all, my attention continued to be focused on Claire, who was nineteen and in her second year of college. Lisa had been diagnosed when Claire was fifteen, and

---

2   **In language perhaps less accessible, psychiatrist Dr. Jorge Isaac Casariego explains** it is important "that a mourner experiences a gradual, normative process of disengagement from the image of the deceased that would additionally help avoid pathological mourning." My layman's translation: it's important to get back into life. Otherwise, you can get stuck mourning someone forever. The seven days of Shiva helps you get back to life by placing a time limit on the formal part of the process. There's a definite end and you are forced to move on when it's over, whether you want to or not.

her entire high school experience and first two years of college were overshadowed by this disease. Lisa was in the hospital and could not attend her high school graduation, and although neither ever complained about it, I know it broke their hearts. It broke mine. Claire spent her first year and a half of college waiting for the phone to ring to tell her that her mother had died. Instead, she was home for winter break of her sophomore year when her mother died in the next room.

I was relieved and so grateful when her two favorite cousins arrived from out of town and slept in her room with her for the entire week. Hearing conversations coming from behind the closed door and even laughter helped me as well. Every evening the house was filled with her elementary and high school friends. Every night there was always a group around Claire. She had gone to an all-girls school and even though they were all young women now, when I looked at them, all I could see were their seven-year-old selves in their navy blue school uniforms with red buttons.

On Friday morning, Claire and I quietly got dressed. Without even thinking, I put on the suit I wore at our wedding and picked out a tie that Lisa bought for me. You look for little things that connect you to the deceased. Claire wore one of Lisa's rings, a pendent and a scarf. We walked the three blocks to our synagogue for the funeral—which would be the main memorial service.

I wish I could remember more of the details of this event, but I can just recall snatches of it. I was just trying to get through it.

Once again, my brain just could not take it all in and there was always this greater sense of disbelief behind it all, the feeling that this couldn't really be happening. All these people couldn't be coming for us, not us. These things happened to *other* people.

I recall the upset look on the faces of various friends. (I have no idea what my own face projected.) I remember greeting almost everyone but, again, it's a blur. I think that's because I have no desire to go back to it in my memory, unlike our wedding, where I have tried to hold on to each moment. Lisa's funeral was something I needed to get through and then file it, never to be revisited. (Just writing the words "Lisa's funeral" is still jarring.)

The service was relatively short. The Rabbi welcomed everyone. Claire read a eulogy she wrote beautifully—an amazingly heartfelt tribute to her mother and their relationship. One phrase stays and still saddens me: "I will be writing my mother's eulogy for the rest of my life."

I could not have stood in front of everyone at nineteen and done what she did. I saw many of her teachers there and was thinking how proud they must have been—sad, but as proud of her as I was. They helped get her there. While she spoke, I couldn't stop focusing on the face of the mother of her best school friend sitting across from me, tears streaming down her cheeks.

I began my eulogy by first thanking everyone for being there and for those who supported and visited Lisa during her illness. I tried to explain what she meant to me and the extraordinary person we all thought she was. I don't think any words could have really accomplished these goals. I'm supposed to be good with words, but on this day, my words felt inadequate.

The Rabbi spoke, he recited the Hebrew prayers, and at the conclusion, Claire and I and Lisa's brother, Jeffrey, stood and recited Kaddish, the Hebrew memorial prayer. Then we walked home where the house was filled with more people than I could ever remember being there at one time.

The Shiva would continue for four more nights with more people coming in and out. On the night after the Shiva officially ended, I was sleeping on the couch in our den—actually, it was more like I was lying on the couch, unable to sleep. I was there because the bed I shared with Lisa was where she'd just died, and I wasn't ready to go back in there just yet.

Among the issues keeping me up (a substantial list), uppermost was Claire's imminent departure back to college in a few hours. I kept thinking of her incredible loneliness on that flight. I was feeling worse and worse until it suddenly felt like Lisa came down and hit me on the head, and said, "Dummy, go with her!"

Of course, I thought. *Duh.*

I went to my computer, made a reservation on the same flight, and felt better immediately. That was Lisa—always the wiser of the two.

Later that morning, we flew back to her college together. I stayed overnight and returned to New York the next morning.

Then came the very worst.

CHAPTER 5

A Haunting Silence

I THOUGHT THINGS WERE BAD before.

But, I had absolutely no idea what was in store for me when I turned the key in the front door and walked back into that empty apartment all by myself.

I was hit with a shattering silence and solitary loneliness the likes of which I had never encountered in my life. Every widow and widower must eventually face this emptiness.

After everyone that filled the house leaves; after all the friends and relatives go back to their homes; after people go back to *their* regular lives, *you* are left all by yourself with something you can't define or even believe.

On one level, you come back thinking: *OK, I've come through the big stuff—illness finally over. Funeral over. Burial over. Shiva over. Daughter back at school. Now I will continue to…what? Where?*

There is nowhere to continue *to* anymore. Unlike everyone who came to the house for the Shiva, I can't leave and go back to my regular life. My regular life has been taken away. That life is over. In a moment, everything, *everything*, has changed.

On one level, I was back in the most familiar place that was so recently full of life, that echoed with endless conversations and laughter and caring and crying and rushed breakfasts getting a child to school, skinned knees, board games, getting dressed up for fancy events, nightly dinners going over the day's events with a glass of wine, birthday parties, holidays, arguments and shouting and intimacy and sex and great joy and love and now…nothing.

A..b..s..o..l..u..t..e..l..y nothing.

Total silence.

I am alone.

At first, it was impossible to even comprehend that this shared space—this shared noisy, busy life—is no longer shared with someone who had as big a stake in it as you. For a while, it's absolutely normal to expect the deceased to walk through the front door, like she did thousands of times before. Even though the rational part of you knows this is not going to happen, you still wait for the sound of the door opening to tell you it's really not true, this isn't really happening. For a long time, I had an honest worry that if I removed anything from her closet, I would face Lisa's wrath, which could be fearsome. When I slowly began the process, I actually had to rationalize it with the thought that if she *did* come back, I would just buy her a new wardrobe and she'd be happy with that. (Seriously. I seriously thought this.)

Slowly, very slowly, you begin to accept that they're not going to walk back in again. It's a realization that whatever this new life is, it has now begun, and you are going to have to figure out some way to live in it. That new clock keeps ticking.

Here was another change that was hard to fathom: this home was now going to be completely my responsibility alone. I would have to make all the decisions and trust me on this, my wife was a complete dictator when it came to everything in the house: its furnishings, its appearance, and, especially, the kitchen. Now I would have to make all these decisions, down to what I would eat for dinner. My free ride was over.

Couples divide up chores. It's normal. One of them is better at or more interested in some household job and divisions are created in a very natural way, almost unnoticed. So, it's a shock when *everything* suddenly falls on the shoulders of the survivor, including the things that he or she ignored up until then. When one partner is a professional, that loss hits you even harder.

I have a friend whose lawyer husband took care of all legal matters (which made sense) and he was smart and aggressive and usually won his cases. Shortly after he died, a property tax issue arose, something he would have handled in a jiffy. Now, she was forced to take a crash course on tax statutes, and even though the rational mind understood it would eventually be resolved, it weighed on her greatly and kept her up at night.

For me, it was anything having to do with medical issues. Lisa was a highly accomplished physician, so I paid zero attention to routine medical questions that came up over the years, especially for Claire. Lisa was on top of it and would simply keep me informed after the fact. One giant reminder of our loss came during that first summer when Claire did something to her foot and it became badly infected. In the past, Lisa would have quietly fixed it and soothed Claire's worry in the most supportive way. Now, I was at a total loss, not because it was an impossible problem to fix, but because it was such a huge reminder of Lisa's absence. Claire later confirmed it was the same with her: her mother's not being there hurt much more than her foot.

We survive. We figure out ways to do the things that were once handled by the departed spouse. But to this day, every time a medical problem arises, there is still a small stab in my heart.

Later, there would be all the official documents surrounding death that the government—state *and* federal— forces us to contend with: an inventory of assets, Letters Testamentary, Letters of Appointment, IRS form SS-4, form 1041, form 8971, and form ET-706, along with the lawyers, the banks, and all the documents that had to be signed, stamped and notarized. I would have to deal with it all, but that could wait.

To add to the horrible silence, the phone stopped ringing. During the Shiva, you kind of get used to the constant knocks at the door. On Day 8, it all stops and it stops abruptly. I assumed well-meaning friends just didn't know if they would be helping or hurting by contacting me. It would have been a huge help if they had, yet at the same time, I didn't reach out to anyone because I didn't want to be perceived as a burden—as the pathetic widower.

Thankfully, there were three people who did not forget me. Lisa's brother and his wife called me every night. So did my kid-sister. They listened to me when I was unhinged and they never criticized.

In all fairness to everyone else, I was not great company at that moment. My mind wandered, it was hard to stay on topic, I couldn't focus, sometimes I cried in public.

I know everyone says it's alright, it's a good thing, "Go ahead, let it out."

That's a lie.

The truth that no one will admit is that it makes people very uncomfortable to watch a grown man cry. It makes everyone uneasy. It shows weakness, a loss of control, and even though we all say it's OK, it's really not. People can't come up with anything to say that will help. (I believe silence is the best way to deal with it, just staying with the person in this silence.) There is one more issue. I don't think I'm a vain person, but my face gets all scrunchy when I cry, really contorted, and I look awful.

Add to this the sense that when I came back to the office or walked into a room or saw people who knew me on the street, many had the same immediate reaction—like there was something wrong with me. I was somehow afflicted, perhaps even contagious. I'd never had that feeling before in my life. I quickly came to detest the long look of pity and I was relieved when I didn't run into anyone.

C. S. Lewis captured this perfectly in his book about his lost wife, *A Grief Observed*, "To some I'm worse than an embarrassment. I am a death's head. Whenever I meet a happily married pair, I can feel them both thinking, 'One or other of us must someday be as he is now.'"[3]

Who wants to be anywhere near that?

Something else slowly began to dawn on me that might sound obvious, but because I had always taken it for granted, I didn't realize its prominence. While I was married to Lisa, I had been strolling through life no longer a lone individual, but part of a luminous couple. I was made logarithmically more dynamic by the addition of this beau-

---

3   C. S. Lewis, *A Grief Observed*, p. 11 Harper San Francisco, 2011.

tiful, accomplished, poised woman at my side. To put it
bluntly, Lisa made me appear better to the outside world.

In the Jewish wedding ceremony, the bride walks
around the groom seven times. There are a number of spiritual interpretations for this public ritual, but there is one
symbolic purpose that I take from it. The bride is staking
her claim over this groom, in front of the entire community. She is saying: "This is my guy. Hands off."

In truth, I loved being *Lisa's guy*. I loved starting a sentence with "My wife says" or "My wife did such and such."
I would often insert her as a foil in columns I wrote for the
paper. I dove into this marriage completely, with my entire
soul. Monogamy certainly doesn't work for everyone, but I
found it enchanting.

Entering a room, a work event, a party, sitting next
to her on an airplane or just strolling down the avenue, I
thought she made me not just better, but more interesting.
To use a celestial metaphor, I had been the moon reflecting
her light and, boy-oh-boy, did she ever cast a radiant glow.

Now, that coveted status had ended. I would, hence-
forth, be judged on my own once again. With Lisa no longer next to me, I felt I was a lesser entity. With the loss of
her illumination, I was left dimmed, diminished.

In my complete arrogance, I had walked through life
assuming this would last forever. I knew bad things cer-

tainly happened, I read about them every day. But they happened to *other* people. Not me.

Perhaps that was the biggest shock. I wasn't special. Even as I write that sentence, even after five years, I still can't believe I'm the guy this happened to.

Talk about an unwillingness to accept reality.

CHAPTER 6

Mr. Fat Penguin

THE KITCHEN COUNTER WAS STILL filled with containers of cookies and cakes that people brought to the Shiva (I was unable to eat any kind of dessert for about three years, probably the only good thing to come from all this).

There were, of course, housekeeping details. Our bathroom cabinet was filled with over 50 bottles of pills along with the medical paraphernalia of her illness throughout the apartment.

The first thing I did—and I did this with a vengeance—was clear the apartment of all medical detritus. The dozens of bottles of pills, the equipment, every reminder of her illness. I've heard other people couldn't remove this stuff fast enough as well.

The illness and all of the paraphernalia that accompanied it were unwelcome intruders and as soon as their role was no longer required, they were banished, hopefully never to return.

But the physical removal is the easy part. The memories of the past four years that were connected to it all, the long days and nights in hospitals, the endless medical appointments, the parade of doctors and nurses in six hospitals in Boston and New York was still with me. Eventually, that would soon disappear as well through the wonderful human ability to block bad events.

I would also have to figure out what to do with what was now *my* bedroom, not *our* bedroom. The mattress was ugly and bare since I had thrown away all the bedding and quilts that were on it when she died. I knew I couldn't sleep on the couch forever, although the thought was tempting. I would eventually buy a new bed and move everything around.

There was, however, one lovely moment on that first night back that brought a rare smile to my face. Before she left for school two days earlier, Claire secretly placed one of her favorite stuffed animals on my pillow on the couch, anticipating my return alone. *Mr. Fat Penguin* gave me an immediate sense of warmth, a reminder that someone in this world still cared about me and he provided some companionship.

My next official task as a widower—throwing out all those damned cookies and cakes.

CHAPTER 7

Some Perspective

THAT WAS ALL FIVE YEARS ago.

The journey from there to here has been one that I could never have even imagined—although there were times during the long hospital stays that I pondered what my life might be like after Lisa died. That was like thinking of infinity—the human mind can only go so far into this realm and then we stop abruptly because we lack the bandwidth.

None of those daydreams of my impending future were accurate. Zero. What actually took place was something I was incapable of knowing. What all widows and widowers face is a new life that is cosmically different from the one before and its very confusing at first. The physical surroundings are all the same, but within this familiar space, the fundamentals have been completely altered. It's a life we obviously didn't want, but, nonetheless, there it is.

Deal with it.

Time to be the adult.

Figure out a way to live in it.

The reason I have written this book is because in those early days after Lisa died, I searched for any kind of reading material that might help guide me through this uncharted terrain. Some people dropped off books by professional grief counselors, psychologists, psychiatrists, clergy. There were pamphlets from the hospice hospital that told me what I already knew, just in fancier language that was harder to understand. There was a paper from Harvard that I found online and purchased for $24.00. Pure academic drivel, totally useless. Perhaps these writings helped others, but they shed no new light for me and gave me no guidance or comfort.

I read Joan Didion's book, *The Year of Magical Thinking*. There were five superb pages that I copied, reread again and again, and have emailed to others who lost a partner (I will quote parts later). But I couldn't relate to the rest of her book, even though I realize others call it the *gold standard* of dealing with grief. One thing though…if Didion meant *crazy thinking* regarding the title, *Magical Thinking*, I believe she was on to something. Luckily, the really crazy thoughts do begin to retreat after about a year, as she implied; more so after two and three years. But their substitutes—loneliness, longing, and sadness—stay forever.

In *A Grief Observed*, C. S. Lewis was so devasted by his wife's death that the great Christian writer seriously questioned his belief in God. "Step by step we were led up the garden path. Time after time, when He seemed most gracious, He was really preparing the next torture." (Lewis rereads this passage the next morning and tries again, but it comes out even worse, suggesting God might be "a Cosmic Sadist or spiteful imbecile."[4] Yikes![5])

Wrestling with God is a common thread in many of these books. People are angry, and who better to direct their anger toward than the One in charge. For me, religion is such an individual preference that I didn't garner any useful guidance from other people's strong beliefs or broken beliefs or no beliefs. I have my own. They are mine. They are strong and they are personal. Period.

But over the past five years, I've received some incredibly insightful emails from friends and had conversations that helped me better understand what had happened. The entire experience forced me to learn something about the world, about human beings, about myself. I won't say I'm a better person for having gone through it. Well, maybe in some ways, but I definitely think I'm wiser. You have to be a real blockhead to go through this and *not* learn something from it. But, what a tough education.

There were certain thoughts, gestures, and kindnesses from friends and strangers that helped enormously. So did just getting up every morning and putting on my

---

4   C. S. Lewis *A Grief Observed*, p. 30. Harper San Francisco, 2011.
5   Me…not Lewis.

socks. And there is that one overused, tired, stale expression—"the passage of time"—one of the most unoriginal phrases, which people assured me from the start would help. I grew really tired of hearing it.

Now, five years later, I have to grudgingly admit I was wrong, there is great truth to it. It turns out the NASA clock has become a friend. The passage of time has, indeed, helped enormously. It allows you to get used to living with it all.

I remember hearing a famous French environmentalist many years ago explain that the real tragedy of human beings is that we get used to bad things like (in his case) an ever-decreasing quality of environment and thus, we allow it to happen. I now believe that's precisely the saving grace of grief. We eventually get used to it, we learn to live with it, and in so doing, its worst parts ease up on us.

It will still crop up out of nowhere and sting you at times. But those moments grow fewer and fewer.

So, in the following pages I will tell you what worked for me and what did not, along with thoughts from others with greater insight than I possess.

I'm not a psychologist. I'm not a medical doctor. I'm not a theologian. I don't presume to know any greater truth here. I am just a very regular guy who had a very bad thing happen to him and I am only slightly ahead of the curve in my generation. Sadly, this will eventually come to everyone and that kind of breaks my heart—knowing all the pain out there yet to come.

After thinking and rethinking all of this, I have arrived at some conclusions that I will share. I hope there is something here that might help you, something you might find useful, because I'm guessing that if you picked this book up in the first place, you are going through a very rough time or about to. It's like nothing you have ever experienced… and, unfortunately, it will never completely go away.

But—and it's an important *but*—five years on, I can write that I am feeling better. That's a sentence I never thought I would write. I feel stronger as well.

The awful moment of walking into the silent apartment is part of my past, along with the long hospital stays and the terrible worry for someone you love who you watch struggling, in pain, and who you can do nothing to help.

I still walk into the same home, but it doesn't hurt anymore. I'm glad, once again, to open the front door. Yes, there are nights when I backslide, but I get past them more quickly now. The acute pain is gone, and most days I am even happy again: looking forward to the day ahead, excited about some event coming up.

By all outward appearances, I seem to be my old self— not just to those around me, but to myself as well.

I can walk down the street on a gorgeous fall day with wonderful music in my AirPods and feel joy. I laugh again and the laughter is real, not forced. I crack jokes that I think are brilliant, and I can enjoy the little ironies that we all encounter every day.

To those around me, my friends, my colleagues, even my daughter, I appear normal, but in one very fundamental way, I am not.

The old me left with my wife. I'm not sure who this new person is—I am still evolving. But I will tell you this with absolute certainty—I am not the same person I was before January 1, 2018.

Not at all.

CHAPTER 8

The Grief Group

EARLY ON, FRIENDS SUGGESTED I might find it helpful to join a group of widows and widowers, a grief group. There was one offered by the hospice that sent nurses to the house in those final two weeks. When I called to register, the social worker running the group explained that she first had to do an "intake," which meant she had to assess my mental status. She asked if it would be alright to ask some personal questions before she let me in.

"No problem," I told her, "Shoot."

"Do you walk into a room and forget why you went?" she began.

"All day long."

"Any changes in your sleep?"

"Yes."

"What are they?"

"I don't sleep much and if I do, I wake up at 4:30 every morning, as if I set an alarm. Coincidently, that's the time my wife died."

"Any changes in weight?

"Yes."

"Up or down?"

"I've lost ten pounds." (I would eventually lose 30 by the summer, putting me at a weight I had not been at since high school, 50 years before. When people told me I looked great, I would respond: "Grief diet. You *really* don't want to try it.")

Then the counselor asked the final question: "Any suicidal thoughts?"

"In my entire life," I told her, "I have never entertained a suicidal thought. Plus, I'm a single parent now and I feel very responsible for my daughter. However, if I got hit by a bus tomorrow and there was a chance that I would see my wife again…well, that would be just fine with me."

"That's not a problem," she told me. "That's a passive suicide thought, not an active one."

Didn't realize there was a difference, but good to know.

Ultimately, the group didn't work for me for two reasons.

First, I felt just awful for everyone there. Seeing the others, hearing their stories, all the tears, made me feel even worse, not better. That, I did not need. My God, there was so much pain in that room you could bottle it.

The second reason it didn't work for me was that the group was composed almost entirely of women. There was a huge imbalance. Out of twelve people, there were ten women and only one other guy in the group besides me.

Granted, we were all going through the same ordeal and shared many of the same heartaches, but there were a lot of issues that were just plain different. The one that dominated for them, the one that came up most often, was the loss of physical protection, which now frightened them. The one person who always protected them was gone, and they talked about this a lot. (In two cases, the dead husbands were policemen, so that kind of made sense.)

Of all the things I missed about Lisa, and there were plenty, physical protection never entered my mind. That's not to say she wouldn't have fought like a banshee if either Claire or I were threatened, it was just something that wasn't very high on my list.

Something I did miss, they never talked about. This may sound trivial, and it was something I took for granted, but there was now a lack of beauty in my life. Lisa was always adding touches to our home that made it lovely. I never paid any attention to the lace towels or the flowers she brought home regularly. I didn't miss them until they weren't there. I tried buying flowers on my own, but that just seemed to compound the problem and made it even worse. It was one more reminder that she wasn't there.

I could spend a chapter on the long list of little things I missed about her. Lisa was constantly buying clothes for our daughter. I didn't have that sense or ability. There was her medical knowledge that I mentioned earlier. She also had a different and keener understanding of people we encountered that I sometimes completely missed. Those observations helped me understand my world in a more nuanced way.

I went to only a few meetings and then I stopped, mostly because I didn't feel better afterwards. But I've thought about those nice ladies, and I hope they are doing better now. I tried to reach out to that other guy, but I lost track of him. I hope he's doing better as well.

CHAPTER 9

Howard's Email

IN THOSE BONE-CRUSHING DAYS SHORTLY after Lisa died, I received an email from my friend, Howard Fillit, that still stands out.

Howard is a geriatrician, an expert in Alzheimer's, and the Chief Science Officer of the ADDF (Alzheimer's Drug Discovery Foundation). More pertinent, Howard lost his wife, who was also a doctor, six years earlier.

I wrote back thanking him for his condolence note and then asked him a brief medical question.

This was Dr. Fillit's response to "How long does it physically hurt?"

It becomes an emotional and psychological scar.

The acute pain of grief and loss turns into a recognition of the magnitude of how life has changed so dramatically.

There are many changes with regard to family and friends, perhaps loneliness, and a loss of self, a loss of who we are.

One has to eventually recreate one's life and a new self. I probably still think of Janet every day. My new life is not what I imagined, or even could have imagined, in any way. Nor is my new self. Although there are remnants deep down inside that haven't changed and have helped me through it all.

Work certainly helps. Eventually life goes on.

It's taken me more than 5 years to really get my emotional bearings back which really surprised me. Functionally I was able to adjust sooner.

I hope you will find some solace and peace and happiness. The wound heals. Let's have lunch!

Howard

I read this over and over, but I could not grasp all its parts when it first arrived in my inbox in those early days. It's taken me five years to fully comprehend the wisdom of this brief, insightful note.

Perhaps it took Howard that long to understand the entire scope as well. I have since shared this with other friends who have lost a spouse. Everyone has commented on how prescient it is—how, in Howard's words, life changes so dramatically.

Yes, we will carry this emotional and psychological scar forever. Yes, there is a loss of self, of who we are, and a struggle to figure out that new self.

My new life is still evolving. Others, I believe, seem to have arrived at their next phase much faster. One friend suggests the journey is like fingerprints—no two are alike.

Oh, I do have lunch with Howard regularly. We compare our progress. It is a friendship I greatly value.

CHAPTER 10

Michael and Harvey

I HAVE TWO FRIENDS WHO lost their wives in the same year I lost Lisa. Michael lost his wife to cancer in July 2018, seven months after Lisa. Harvey lost his wife a month later, in August 2018.

I was in email contact with Michael, who lives in another state. About three months after his wife died, I called one Sunday afternoon to say hello. I expected to find someone in a deep hole, which is where I remained. But his voice was steady, and he even sounded fairly upbeat. Near the end of the conversation, he somewhat sheepishly told me that he had *met* someone.

I was a little surprised, but I supported him completely, saying, "That's great, good for you." I meant it too.

He explained that very shortly after the funeral, as he was cleaning out the house, he dropped off some of his late wife's art supplies at the home of a woman he vaguely knew. They wound up having a long talk and then dinner. That continued and he was now seeing a great deal of her.

Not too long after our phone call, he sold his home and moved in with her, and they are now married. When he told me his sons were upset that he had moved on so quickly, I reminded him that he had been a devoted husband and he supported his wife throughout her illness. He had nothing to answer to anyone. I was also slightly jealous. I jokingly told him that in the small town where they live, he might pass 25 people a day. In New York, I pass 2,500… and he's the one who found someone!

This past spring, I met Michael and his wife, Ann. He is happy. They are happy together. They travel. They are taking dance lessons. By all outward appearances, Michael is doing great.

The other man, Harvey, lives near me, and we get together for a beer every few months to compare notes. Within the first year, some friends wanted him to meet a woman who lived in a nearby city. They began with long phone conversations and then started seeing each other. Within two years, he sold his apartment, they bought a new home together and have married.

Both Michael and Harvey suffered the same huge loss, but they were able to move forward much more quickly than I. They also seem to be very happy. Even though I said at the outset that there is no one prescription for everyone, their ability to move on has made me question myself and my inability to move ahead successfully.

There are other stories as well. My friend Adam's experience has been more complicated.

CHAPTER 11

Even After 50 Years!

ADAM S IS A LONGTIME friend who is a bit older. He's been retired for years but keeps very busy on the boards of non-profits. He also looks and sounds much younger than his age. If you are on his email list, you will receive between 15 and 20 emails from him every day on a variety of l issues – all of them worthwhile (except his jokes).

I also know Adam's lovely wife of more than 50 years, Marion, and I've met their four grown children. Adam had a first wife who died shortly after his oldest child was born. We never talked about it and his daughter has only known Marion as her mother.

Shortly after Lisa died, I received this email from Adam in response to the same question I asked Howard:

Hi Warren,

I have personal answers to your question, but they were custom-made for me. Everyone who gets hurt this way gets their own personal answers. I suspect none of them are the same. This is for a talk over a cup of coffee, not an email. But I can tell you one thing. It hurts me to write this email. Not the same hurt as long ago. It's a hurt which simply becomes a companion. Sometimes unfelt. Sometimes front and center. Time does help. How much is like your fingerprints. No one else has them and no one else will feel just as you do as time passes.

The good news? Lives get put back together. Some really well. Some just OK. That is, from my own experience, a pure, unadulterated function of the mental toughness and resilience of the individual, coupled with unpredictable things and people which/who will bump into you as you go along—i.e., luck. Some of that you can manufacture yourself and some of it just happens.

Advice? Be tough and hard on yourself. I got a C+ or maybe a B- on that score. My dad saw it and tried to tell me, but I only heard someone sounding unsympathetic and I got angry with him—and he wasn't a good enough communicator to get inside my head and help me internalize what he was telling me. Absolutely none of my friends ever was anything other than caring and kind and sympathetic.

Looking back 50 years now, it might have helped if one of them had told me what my dad tried to

*tell me. The only absolute here is that the Adam S.
who existed before that loss disappeared with it. The
Adam S. who continued afterwards is a very different person. I didn't know much about anything, so I
didn't look for support/advice from others who had
had a similar loss, or professionally. I just slogged
through it.*

*We can talk about it all when we see each other. I
didn't intend to write this. It just came out.*

See you very soon, Warren.

Adam

I was struck by what Adam wrote, his insight and his
caring, but I put it away for more than four years. Last fall,
I came across it again by accident. So, four years later, I
asked if we could finally have that much delayed cup of coffee. We sat down in a lovely outdoor café on Broadway on
a beautiful fall afternoon. The conversation that ensued is
the genesis of this book.

I began by showing him the email that he sent four
years earlier. He sat across from me and read it silently on
my phone. When he finished, he looked up at me nodding.

"I don't even know your first wife's name," I said.

"It was Liz," he said quietly.

"When were you married?"

He struggled remembering the exact year because he hadn't thought about it in so long.

"We got married in 1965."

I asked what happened.

What came forth was an excruciating story of a young woman who had just given birth to their first child, a healthy daughter, and then, through a medical mistake, died shortly afterwards in terrible pain. So many of us think about maternal deaths as something from another century, but they are still very real—over 300,000 women per year worldwide and over 1,000 in the US.

Adam was a young man with a demanding job, and he now had a newborn to take care of and was dealing with his own enormous heartbreak.

As bad as things were for me, my daughter was nineteen, and my wife had had a monumental influence on her childhood and her teenage years. I didn't have to raise an infant on my own while holding down a high-pressured job. Plus, Claire would always remember her mother. For Adam's daughter, her birth mother would forever be a mystery.

Adam was also lucky. He met Marion within six months, and she was willing to take on a grieving widower with an infant. They built a wonderful life together and a new family and have had great adventures all over the world.

But when I sat with Adam and asked him about his late wife, something changed in him, and he was an Adam I had never seen before. It reminded me of interviews I had done with veterans when they talked about their war experiences. I felt awful bringing this all up again because it was something he had suppressed for fifty years, and it was something—even with the joy of his marriage to Marion—that has never gone away.

We talk to people every day. Most conversations are not memorable. But there are a few, a very few, that are profound. You know it when it happens. My conversation with Adam on that beautiful fall afternoon over that cup of coffee at an outdoor café on Broadway was profound.

It was hard for him to tell his story and it was hard for me to hear it. Throughout, I kept thinking, *Even after all these years.* Later that same afternoon, this email came in.

Warren,

Thanks for today—the food included.

When I had my cardiac ablations, they went inside the chambers of my heart with catheters, one of which emits radio frequency waves (RFW). After computer mapping the electrical system of my heart, they identified the places where the errant signals were coming from and they "burned" them with the RFWs. The scar tissue which formed then blocks these errant signals, eliminating the a-fib.

That metaphor popped into my head when I read the word "scar" in Howard Fillit's note to you (which I had sent to him).

In a way, that's what happens to us over time—some longer, others less so—with the wounds we have suffered. Trouble is, if the heart operation is a success, the errant signals are permanently blocked.

For me, since there are no radio frequency waves to permanently block my pain, I've substituted a form of amnesia as a "treatment." As I said today, it works OK in stopping the pain, but it doesn't block the emotional "signals," so I have been left with those, but without a day-to-day consciousness of why I have them.

Today's talk was kind of cathartic, Warren, and probably good for me. One can't shake the emotional baggage on a daily basis if you don't remember where it's coming from. What I've discovered is that because it is so free-floating, I have unconsciously attached it to other things which, while upsetting, oughtn't make me down as often as I am. If I can remember where these signals are originating, I can consciously take my father's poorly expressed, but good, advice and move around them.

In my talks with Bob C., the shrink friend I told you about, when he said I wasn't depressed, I was sad. It was in the context of my talking to him about all the things around me which were upsetting. He pointed out that I was attaching my "free-floating" sadness to things which I logically deserved to be upset about, which weren't the real cause. He actually said that if I was less smart, I'd be better able to identify the actual source, but I am clever enough to find logical things to be upset about so I am able to avoid confronting what has remained so difficult for me.

Huh. This email is turning out to be about me which wasn't my intention.

As I think I said in my past email which you had on your phone, we are all unique and while there are excellent generalizations which fit almost all of us— as Howard properly says—each individual person has his/her own unique emotional and psychological responses to this kind of trauma. We're all alike in so many ways, but like fingerprints, no one else has the same ones and I believe every person who has suffered the kind of trauma we are speaking about, has particular "long symptoms" to deal with forever. Stupid COVID has provided me with a new way of saying that it has lasted for me.

In the end, you get "lucky"—sooner or later—and find what you need so much in another person. But the Adam S or Warren Kozak they fall for isn't the same guy with the same name he was before the trauma. Part of it I think is whether the lucky lady understands what we will always have inside and knows how to be what we need without feeling as if she is competing with the lady who came before.

I'm rambling, I know. But our talk today has left me with a lot to think about and deal with. Tearing away scar tissue can help in the end, but it hurts when it happens. And what I am particularly surprised about is that Bob C.'s insights so many years ago, which made perfect sense to me at the time, until today, I also seem to have pushed behind my protective wall.

I got very lucky with Marion who, as a really young woman, not only became a mother overnight but was able to deal with my ex-in-laws in my stead because I simply couldn't. Her strength and understanding were extraordinary.

You'll get "lucky," also. Maybe in a "usual" way with a friend's introduction, or maybe by complete happenstance.

Sorry about this email's length. See you soon.

Adam

After fifty years, a happy marriage, four kids, and a very successful and impressive career, it still hurts, and it never completely goes away.

I think the analogy I made earlier to veterans is correct. You carry this experience with you until your dying day. How you deal with it throughout the rest of your life depends on a number of factors: good counseling, the love of family and friends, perhaps religious guidance, a personal understanding of the experience, a new love, and more.

What doesn't work is to ignore the magnitude of the loss. Something happened and it was a very big deal.

CHAPTER 12

How Many Are We Talking About?

THERE ARE 3,700,000 WIDOWERS TODAY in the United States and three times the number of widows—11,480,000. Combining both genders, that comes to about 6 percent of the US population. Those numbers will increase rapidly over the next two decades as the Baby-Boom generation takes its exit. (Which can't come soon enough according to some Millennials.)

The average age of widows is 59 years—younger than I would have guessed. Here's a strange fact—the state with the highest number of widows per capita? West Virginia. The lowest? Alaska. (Marriage seems to last longer in long, cold winter nights. Or people do.)

In the first six months after losing a spouse, there is a 61 percent greater likelihood of death for the survivor versus the general population. Recent studies show the number one factor that keeps people living longer is not quitting smoking, or exercise, although both help a lot. The number one factor is connection with other human beings. I was lucky during the entire first year. Lisa's brother and his wife phoned me every night during those first few months and listened to me cry and tell the same stories about his sister every night. My younger sister was also there to listen to me. These people, along with my friends, helped keep me alive.

There is one huge difference between the genders: remarriage. After losing a spouse, 20 percent of older men remarry, while only 2 percent of women do the same.

One widow told me, with more than a little resentment, that "women grieve, while men remarry." Although those numbers back her up, I'm not sure how one can quantify anyone else's level of grief. It may not be right or fair, but it's true that it's more socially acceptable for men to date younger women while the number of men in, say, their fifties who want to date a woman in her seventies or eighties is lower. There is no question that there is still a basic unfairness between the sexes when it comes to finding new partners. On the other hand, I don't think men grieve any less than women.

One last thought on the topic—an article in the *New York Times* that received a great deal of attention examined the new phenomenon of elderly single people (made single by either death and divorce) who are in committed relationships, but keeping their apartments, not marrying and not combining assets. Instead of living together, they are together two, three, or four nights a week, but go back to their own space on the other nights.

The people interviewed for the article show no less commitment to each other. I believe this would be more popular with the population that reads the *New York Times* than, say, other folks, who might not have the means to maintain two or even more residences.

I will leave you with one last number that is slightly more positive: approximately 29 percent of all widowers will get into a new relationship after the death of their spouse. Seven percent of widows will do the same. The numbers are still vastly uneven…but it's better than the 2 percent of women who remarry.

CHAPTER 13

Crying Underwater

I USED TO WONDER IF I had a personality defect because I rarely, if ever, cried. I was very close to my grandmother and when she died suddenly, I felt terrible, but I didn't cry. The same with my parents years later.

After Lisa died, especially in that first year, I made up for all previous years everywhere and all the time. I would lose control of my emotions in very uncomfortable places.

More than once, it happened on the subway, and I began to wear sunglasses at times, making me look like one of those guys inside the car who always gave me the creeps. I would cry walking down the street in New York, on the elliptical at the gym, sometimes at work events when I would quickly excuse myself, go to the bathroom, and shut the door in the stall.

During the first year of mourning, a Jew is required to recite Kaddish, at the end of every service for just shy of twelve months. (After that year of mourning, Kaddish is recited only on the anniversary of the death.) There is a group of mostly orthodox guys that came together in a nearby office for afternoon prayers and I would join them.

Kaddish always concludes the service. There is a rhythm, a cadence to it that is familiar to any Jewish person who has ever walked into a synagogue.

One day in the afternoon group—and this was already half a year on—for no reason I could ascertain, I just burst into tears right in the middle of reciting Kaddish. It was an enormous struggle just to get through it. As much as I tried, I could not regain my composure and kept breaking down in tears. When I finally finished, I looked up and everyone in the room was just staring at me in silence, some with their jaws open. I don't think it was with disdain. I believe I saw concern, perhaps empathy. Some came over afterward and put their hand on my shoulder. I gave them a forced smile as a way of acknowledgment. But I'm guessing they had never seen that before. I sure hadn't.

By that point, I was beyond embarrassment over this sort of thing. It was just part of this new territory. I didn't know when it would hit or what brought it on at that particular time.

In the first summer after Lisa died, I was at our lake house in Wisconsin, mostly by myself. I have a morning ritual out there that I never change. The first thing I do when I wake up is go for a long swim, no matter how cold it is, followed by a pot of hot coffee. That first summer, all I could think of during those swims was Lisa. When I was doing the backstroke, I would look up at the big sky and huge clouds and wonder where she was. I wondered if she was looking back down on me. She was on my mind the entire way.

One day, when I was doing the crawl, I just burst into tears—never a great idea when your head is underwater. Then, I started to laugh at the ridiculousness of crying underwater. Laughing is an equally unwise idea with your head submerged. At that point I stopped, treaded water, and then just headed back to shore for coffee.

Beautiful sad songs on Spotify would cause me to burst into tears when I was rowing on the lake, or walking down the street in Manhattan with my AirPods in my ears. I had no idea there were so many beautiful songs, truly beautiful, that are also so sad. In the past, I guess I never paid attention to the lyrics. Now they had a deeper meaning, or I had a deeper understanding.

I began to gain control of my emotions after a year. It was better in the second year and better still in the third. Now, five years later, when I take those swims, I just concentrate on my strokes or how cold it is. Lisa is not part of it.

Five years on, it still happens. I still cry, but with much less frequency. It's often brought on by music or someone's kindness, or for reasons I don't understand. Only now, it's more like a sneeze. I can feel it coming on, and the duration is about the same. Thankfully, even this happens less and less every day.

CHAPTER 14

Short Takes

WHAT *NOT* TO SAY

ONE MORNING SHORTLY AFTER THE funeral, I was on the elevator of my building and a woman who lives on another floor got on. When she saw me, she started to naturally smile and say good morning, but then she suddenly remembered. She put on that long face I would grow to hate and said: "I'm sorry to hear about your wife. I know what it's like...my mother died." (It could've been a lot worse. A college acquaintance of Claire's said she seemed "a little" down. When Claire explained that her mother had recently died, the girl said she understood: "My dog died.")

I learned a lesson from my brief encounter in the elevator. Thereafter, whenever I reached out to people who lost someone, I made sure I never presumed to know what they were going through or compare their loss to my own. If they knew my history, they understood this was something we shared. If they did not know me well, I did not need to tell them that it happened to me too.

୫୬୯ଓ

CHANGING A PASSWORD

In those early days when I started the paperwork of death, one of the first items was changing our Amazon password. It was tied to Lisa's credit card, now canceled. I didn't give it much thought until two hours later, I received a panic call from Claire at college.

"What happened to Mommy's password?" she cried. "Why was she removed from the account?"

I explained why it was necessary to change the credit card if we were going to continue to use Amazon. I quickly gave her the new password. But it dawned on me—here was something new…a 21st -century marker of death. One more reminder for this nineteen-year-old college student, on what might have otherwise been a nice afternoon, that her mother was gone. And all she was doing was trying to buy something on Amazon.

৪৩৪৪

THANKS, I GUESS

I was in a restaurant with my friends Doug and Dalya Woodham.

We were talking about pretty much everything when Dalya offered an observation.

"I know you are not ready for this," she said, "but when you are, you are going to be a hot commodity."

Beating me to it, her husband asked: "What makes Warren a hot commodity?"

To which Dalya replied, "Well, for starters, he's breathing."

Always setting a high bar.

৪৩৫৪

A NIGHT ON THE TOWN

Early on, I went out to a fascinating dinner in an elegant setting in Manhattan. Trust me, there weren't that many in that first year. On this particular night, there was a very engaging speaker. The other guests at my table were stimulating. I walked out afterwards on a remarkably clear night in New York. The skyscrapers sparkled like diamonds. I was reminded why I moved here after college almost 50 years before and I remembered that life can be exciting. "Look at fancy me…toast of the town."

Then I went home and all I could think of was how much Lisa would have enjoyed the evening, how much I would have enjoyed being with her, how I would have loved going over all the little details with her when we got home.

Instead, I had no one to share it with. I was all alone.

৪৩৫৪

SOME UNSOLICITED ADVICE

I was coming into my office building in mid-town Manhattan a few months after Lisa died when I saw my boss's brother on his way out. When he realized it was me, he came across the lobby. He uses a cane now and you could hear the *tap...tap...tap* as he made his way over to me. This man lost his wife of almost sixty years and was now happily remarried.

He came up to me, he put his finger in my chest and just said: "J-Date (A dating site for Jewish singles) ...get on it NOW!"

I rolled my eyes and said: "Leonard, I am *not* going on J-Date."

"If you don't," he replied, "you'll be dead in three years!"

When I got upstairs, the first person I saw was my boss and I said: "You won't believe what your brother just told me."

After I shared the exchange, he thought about it for a moment and then responded: "You don't have to go on J-Date."

Then, showing both kindness and concern, he added:

"But if you're lonely in six months, let's revisit it."

༄༅༄

TWO DIRECTIVES

Lisa could not discuss her impending death, but sometimes it would come out in fleeting thoughts when you least expected it. One day, we were sitting quietly in her hospital room. I was reading something, and she was looking at her iPad. Out of the blue, she said: "You know, it's said that if you had a good marriage, it will be easier moving on to another relationship."

I understood exactly what she was telling me. In the most gracious way, she was giving me permission and even encouraging me to move on after she was gone.

Now it was I who couldn't deal with this conversation, and I told her I would not discuss it. But after a pause, I realized shutting her down was wrong and I wanted to be gracious and acknowledge her kindness. So, I reversed her thought.

"OK, if something happened to me," I replied, "would I want you going into a nunnery? ...I guess not," I said, answering my own question. "That wouldn't be right. But you absolutely cannot have sex with anyone else in the boathouse in Wisconsin. That is *my* turf! You even try that, lady, and I will personally come back down and throw lightning bolts at both of you!"

I got a smile out of her, which made me feel good.

She offered one more directive sometime later.

"I know you," she told me. "Don't save every dime for Claire. It won't be good for her...or for you. Spend some money on yourself. Buy some new clothes."

This was an ongoing issue in our marriage. Lisa never had a problem spending money. I did. She bought beautiful clothes. She filled the house with expensive things. She pushed me to go on trips that I complained about and then enjoyed thoroughly.

Her second directive has been harder to follow.

ಹಿ∞

SIZE 9

Lisa had many, many boxes of shoes. God knows how much money she spent on all of these. Unfortunately, Claire had a different shoe size, so there was no point in keeping them. But I didn't want to give them away to strangers.

I quietly asked various women I knew, including everyone in my office, what their shoe size was. No one had it.

Then one day, I was talking with a young woman we knew and liked very much, who was in medical school here. I discovered something strange: she not only shared Lisa's birthday but had the same shoe size as well.

She came by and was thrilled as she went through what amounted to a treasure trove of shoes, some worn only once.

I helped her carry many shopping bags to an Uber and for some reason, it meant a great deal to me knowing that someone Lisa liked so much would be wearing her shoes, especially on medical rounds.

But one thing happened during this experience that I found upsetting. When our friend was trying on each pair, I realized I had never noticed any of them on Lisa. None of them looked familiar. When Lisa and I went out, I was always dazzled by the entire package, but I didn't remember any of the details…especially what shoes she wore.

I wish I had been a little more observant, and I felt lousy, considering all the effort Lisa put into looking so wonderful.

But, that afternoon, I was very happy to see them go to someone Lisa liked so much. For some reason, wearing her shoes struck me as deeply personal.

୫ୠଔଔ

A NEW COOKBOOK

At the check-out counter at Trader Joe's one morning, the young lady behind the register looked at my shopping cart and said: "I have never seen a customer buy so many bottles of salsa."

I just smiled and didn't say this was the *Lonely Widower's Cookbook*. I had discovered that if I took any leftovers in the refrigerator, put everything in a large bowl, and mixed in enough salsa for flavor, that became dinner. Sometimes, I just filled a Tupperware container with the leftover lunch they served in my office, added salsa, and voila…dinner.

Lisa was an inspired, amazingly creative chef. In spite of long hours at her job and taking care of our home and our daughter, she also managed almost every night to make the most amazing and creative dinners. She would work out on the elliptical at the gym watching the Food Channel. When a recipe caught her attention, she would change it with what she thought might work even better and the three of us had five-star dinners almost every night.

The checkout counter was just one more reminder of how much my life had so dramatically changed. My interest in food left with her.

8003

SEARCHING FOR SOMETHING

Three months after Lisa died, I started the process of going through her drawers. I found a pair of TED stockings, the full-length pressure stockings she wore near the end because of heart failure. Those stockings went onto her legs with greater ease as the disease progressed and she became more skeletal.

Before I threw them out, I put them in my face to breathe in her smell, which was vanishing along with her.

೮೦೧೮

A SIMPLE QUESTION

I was having lunch with my friend, Tom, about four months after Lisa died. He asked an intriguing question: Who's your next of kin?

I suddenly realized that had changed as well. "I guess it's my daughter," I told him, but it put one more exclamation point on everything. My next of kin, my closest relation, my power of attorney, my medical power of attorney…they were all gone, and all this paperwork had to be changed.

೮೦೧೮

MY DATE IN TEL AVIV

A year and a half after Lisa died, I was in Israel for work and brought Claire along. A close friend suggested I meet someone he knew for dinner as a possible new person in my life. I told him this was probably not a good idea right now. I really wasn't ready, plus, even if I were interested, there would be a bit of a distance issue. He still pushed, and I told him I was there with my daughter.

"So, bring her along." I love Israeli practicality.

On our last night, Claire and I met the lady for dinner. She was very nice and we got to see a different part of Tel Aviv. When we were finished, we said goodnight and Claire and I decided to walk back to our hotel.

As we walked back, Claire asked if she could make some observations.

"Sure," I said, not knowing what to expect. "Go ahead.".

"Well, first of all, you weren't interested in her."

I was surprised because it was true.

"But, someday," she continued, "you *will* meet someone you are interested in. When that happens, you shouldn't mention Mommy ten times in the conversation. It makes them feel self-conscious."

Sound, intelligent dating advice from someone I once diapered. One more indication of the strange turn my life had taken.

৪০೮৪

MY GERMAN FRIEND

On my first work trip to Europe after the funeral, I was in Berlin for about four days. The head of our European office is someone I know quite well and consider a good friend. We've had dinner together in various countries over the years, and he'd met Lisa. So when I first saw him, I was surprised he said absolutely nothing, no words of condolence. I remember thinking, *Well, maybe Germans are different about this.*

At that first meeting, we were sitting at a large conference table and he waited after it was over until everyone else got up and left the room.

As soon as we were alone, he turned to me and asked, simply:

"Zo, how are you today? Shitty…or *really* shitty?"

It was one of the most honest and appreciated condolences I received.

ಬ☯ಚ

SOCIAL MEDIA DOESN'T HELP

There is a tradition among Hasidic and Orthodox Jews: no public displays of affection. You will never see a Hasidic couple walking down the street holding hands or, God forbid, kissing on the street. Ever wonder why they don't do this?

The reason is really quite lovely. Besides being socially circumspect, they are also aware that there are people in the world who don't have someone in their lives and they don't want to make them feel worse or more alone.

I became more aware of this after I lost Lisa and I began to notice friends on Facebook posting photos on their happy anniversaries—thirty year, forty years, whatever.

While I completely understood this and I didn't begrudge their joy, it also hurts.

I spend less time on social media now.

৪০৫৪

DARK, BUT FUNNY

During her final hospital stay, I put Lisa in a special wing where she could have a private room. There was an odd billing system for this room. Instead of taking care of everything when she was discharged, I had to go to the business office and pay for this room every day she was there. I came to know the people at the desk, and they always asked how she was doing.

One day, I had to leave Lisa earlier than usual to get to my office for a meeting and I stopped by to pay on my way out. There was a different person at the desk. Without asking, he gave me three new forms to sign. I didn't understand and said I never had to sign any forms before.

"Is this new?" I asked.

"We've always done it this way," he explained. "We won't release the body until all three forms are signed."

I looked at him and said, "My wife has cancer and she isn't doing well, but I just left her two minutes ago and I'm pretty sure she was still breathing."

The man looked terribly embarrassed.

"I'm so sorry," he said. "It's just that the only people who ever come in here wearing suits and ties are undertakers."

⬧⬥⬧

A DINNER IN MOSCOW

I was at a work dinner in Moscow with an Israeli photographer friend and two Russian women who worked for our counterpart there.

During our conversation, it came out that both of the women and my friend were all three divorced. One of the women then turned to me and asked if I was married.

The question, which was a reasonable one, caught me off guard because no one had asked me that in more than twenty years. I had taken off my wedding ring in increments over the previous year, first just during the day, while still wearing it at night. Finally, I kept it off altogether. I suppose I wasn't exactly sure what my status was in my own mind.

"There's a question," I said. "The strange thing is that I still *feel* very married, but I guess I'm not anymore."

They looked at me quizzically as I then explained, "My wife died last year."

They looked stunned and upset by this news, so I tried to lighten the mood.

"I'm afraid our table is not a good advertisement for marriage," I explained. "Even when it works, it doesn't work."

But that was the first time I realized something fundamental: I was no longer legally married.

༄༅

THIS DIDN'T HELP

In that first year, my college roommate and his wife mentioned that they signed up for a trip to see Antarctica with an organization called Road Scholar, formerly Elderhostel. After thinking about this, I called them back and asked if it would be OK if I tagged along. They were thrilled and I thought this would force me back into the world. It was a big step. I asked my boss if he minded my taking the time off and he could not have been more encouraging. "I'll drive you to the airport," he said.

I looked up the trip on the organization's website, studied the configuration of the ship, and called to book a cabin. A nice associate on the phone went over the details. I told him the cabin range I was interested in and he said there was still availability. We proceeded almost until the end when he asked for the name of the other person I would be traveling with.

I explained I would be by myself.

"Oh, I'm afraid these are double rooms."

I told him I understood that and I would pay the cost of the double.

Warren Kozak

"I'm sorry," he said. "We need to have the exact number of slots filled for activities and although there are a few single rooms, there are very few of them and they sell out quickly."

Maybe this came on a bad day, but I felt as if I had been punched in the gut, like there was a huge neon sign over my head flashing: "Widower...widower...widower."

I hadn't felt this rejected since high school.

The guy offered one unhelpful suggestion, "Why don't you go out to a bar tonight, find a beer buddy, and bring them along?"

What an idiot.

❧☙

A CUSTOMER FOR LIFE

I told you about the bed and the bedroom.

Shortly after Lisa died, I called the Saatva mattress company where we had recently purchased our mattress. I explained that I needed to replace it and would like to get the same one again.

The lady looked at our record and realized we had just purchased it. She asked what the problem with it was.

I explained there was nothing wrong with the mattress, I just needed to get a new one.

She asked why.

There was a long pause. I couldn't and didn't want to make up a lie, so I told her the truth.

"My wife had been sick," I explained. "That's why we bought this mattress…to make it more comfortable for her to sleep. It is a very good mattress and it helped. But she died in the bed last week and I need to get a new one for myself."

Silence. Then she asked if I would mind holding for a moment. When she came back on, she said, "We'll send a new one." And then she stunned me when she said, "We will only charge you our cost," which was a fraction of the price.

They certainly did not have to do this, and I did not always find this kind of compassion. But I can't say enough about this company. I am still very moved by what Saatva did.

༄༅

AHEM…

One last note on the bedroom: Shortly after Lisa died, there was a wonderful lady that a friend recommended to help make some changes in the apartment. When she walked in, she always brought sunshine. Really great ideas. She was kind. Happy. Supportive. Fun. Some people have positive energy. She had it in spades.

But when we walked into the bedroom, she looked around and the first thing she noticed were all the photos I recently framed and put all over the room: Lisa, Lisa and Claire, Lisa and me, the three of us. I will grant you, I may have gone overboard.

"Warren," she asked, "do you have any albums?"

"Of course I have albums," I answered.

"Well," she replied, waving her arm across the room, "take *all* of these photos down and put them in your albums…. Otherwise, you are never going to get laid again."

৮৩৫৪

MY FAVORITE STORY IN THAT FIRST YEAR

After Lisa died, I started traveling again for work. In the past, as soon as my assignment was finished, I returned home as quickly as possible to be with Lisa and Claire. Now, there was no one to come home to, so it dawned on me that I could actually stay an extra day or two to take advantage of where I was.

I happened to be in Brussels about one year later. After I finished there, I took the train to Paris and stayed with close friends for the weekend. Coincidentally, this fell on our wedding anniversary, which could have been a difficult time, but it wasn't. I loved seeing my friends and I walked all over the city, went to museums, bought the most expensive and fanciest cookie in history, and did all the tourist things people do.

When I boarded the plane to leave, I happened to sit next to a woman in business class. It turned out that her family owned a wine company and had vineyards all over the world. When it became apparent that I knew nothing about wine and had even less interest, the conversation kind of petered out. When we landed in New York, I wished her well and she did the same.

But as I was walking towards passport control, I noticed her next to me and she was laughing, so I asked what was so funny. As we walked together, she explained that she takes this Paris-to-New York flight often and on her last flight she said she sat next to "a nice man like you."

"We didn't talk much," she said. "He helped me with my bag, but as we were walking down this corridor, I had the odd feeling that people were staring at me. And when we got into passport control, everyone started yelling."

It turned out this woman sat next to Bruce Springsteen for nine hours and had no clue. I love this story, it gave me a laugh and, yes, even though I thought about Lisa through-out the weekend, I saw it as a start. I enjoyed myself.

I was getting back on the bicycle after a rough fall. I got through it, and I even had a great story to tell.

CHAPTER 15

Imagined Scenarios and Reality

I HAVE KEPT A DIARY for most of my adult life. I began in 1980 when I was traveling so much, I couldn't keep track of the cities I was in. Then, it became a habit. Five years after Lisa died, I felt the need to look at my entries from the last year of her life and the time shortly afterwards. It may have been a way for me to reconnect with her, the time when I last saw her, when we last spoke. It could have also been an attempt to better understand everything that happened now that I possessed some hindsight.

This shouldn't have surprised me, but it did—how truly difficult her illness really was. I knew it was bad, but I had clearly forgotten most of it, or blocked it.

Between Lisa's constant medical issues, the psychological strain of her impending death, all the doctors, the hospitals, the screw-ups, the waiting rooms, trying to take care of Claire's needs as she was finishing high school and starting college and trying to do a halfway decent job at work, which could be demanding—with all of this going on, I could not dwell on any of the details at the time. I was just trying to get through each day.

Reading it all five years later, it just seemed like one crisis after another. And overshadowing every crisis was the understanding that these would be the last days I would spend with Lisa. *Not* remembering any of this in detail was both a necessity and a blessing.

But looking at it all again forced me to remember. Some of the moments are still quite clear, especially the feeling I had when I left the different hospitals late at night in summer, fall and in winter and just gulped down the fresh air as soon as I stepped outside, feeling like I had been released from a prison. There was also the guilt knowing Lisa was still inside, breathing the stale air, surrounded by beeping machines and constant interruptions to keep her from sleeping, not to mention the pain she was in. More than once, as I walked outside feeling released, I wondered why I was the healthy one? Why was I able to escape for a few hours?

During those long days in the hospital, when our lives were completely disrupted and any semblance of a personal life was taken away, I tried to imagine future scenarios after this was all over.

I envisioned myself coming home from work and reading all the books I couldn't read during her illness.

I even kept Claire's high school textbooks on algebra, biology, and earth science, so I could reacquaint myself with these topics. (They remain on the bookshelf, unopened.)

I thought I would immediately restart a book I had set aside and finally finish it. It remains untouched and unfinished.

Because I had no time for myself, I thought I would start going out again and seeing friends, going to talks and cultural events. Restarting a social life.

In reality, after Lisa's death, I was so desolate I could barely function. For the first two years, I stayed home most nights by myself, unless I was invited out, which didn't happen too often.

I clearly wasn't all together. Even I knew this. I had a hard time sitting at a dinner table following the conversations because of distracted thoughts, like, *What if Lisa were here with me? Why isn't she here? Where is she? Why did this happen to her...to me?* Self-pity is a real issue.

After her death, my evenings consisted of coming home alone, not having much appetite for dinner, and eventually looking at photos and videos of our happy life together before her diagnosis. Now, when photos mysteriously pop up on my iPhone, I categorize them as *Pre-Diagnosis* and *Post-Diagnosis*. The *before* and *after* of my life.

I also began to develop a less than honest memory of Lisa. She became unrealistically perfect as time took her further from me. Somehow, the normal arguments that we had in our marriage disappeared. I remembered her as being all good, which, of course, she was not. None of us are.

The biggest surprise was the change in my brain function and I believe this was why I thought I would be so energetic and creative after her death. During her illness, I was hyper-efficient. I did a fairly good job at everything. I know I published some of my best pieces—often writing in a hospital room.

However, *after* she died, my brain just went out to lunch. My attention span evaporated. I could barely do my work. Everything was an effort and it wasn't my best. All those books I was going to read? I couldn't get past the second page.

C. S. Lewis called it the laziness of grief. "I loathe the slightest effort. Not only writing but even reading a letter is too much. Even shaving… It's easy to see why the lonely become untidy, finally dirty and disgusting."[6] (Thankfully, unlike Lewis, I showered and shaved.)

One quote in the Didion book resonated: "After a year," a friend told Joan Didion, "I could read headlines."[7]

In my case, it took even longer. I struggled to get through an entire article and retain its points. I was fascinated by this complete change in my brain function

---

6   C.S. Lewis, *A Grief Observed,* p. 5. Harper San Francisco, 1961.
7   Joan Didion, *The Year of Magical Thinking,* p. 47. Random House, 2005.

before and after her death. Veterans have told me about their struggles with post-traumatic stress—how they could function in battle, but once back home, normal life became a challenge. The scene in *The Hurt Locker* that takes place in the cereal aisle is something many can relate to. Buying Corn Flakes becomes a challenge. Corn Flakes!

The brain comes back eventually, but it comes back in increments, and it comes back slowly.

Yes, we are the same person with the same brain. But in the end, we are not the same.

CHAPTER 16

The Elevator Pitch

YEARS BEFORE, LISA AND I attended a book launch party at an apartment in New York. As we left, a woman joined us in the hall to wait for the elevator. We introduced ourselves as we got on and she explained that she was a book promoter. I told her that my first book was about to come out in two months and asked if she had any advice.

"Yes," she said without hesitation, "the people you expect to help won't, and the people you least expect to help, will."

The doors opened in the lobby and she walked away.

For years after, Lisa and I called her the *Apparition*, because that small bit of wisdom came true not just with the book publication, but in other aspects of our lives. During Lisa's illness and after her death, the Apparition's prediction was never more apparent. Some friends were consistent and true, but some absolutely disappeared. There were people who came to our home often and we included in our family celebrations. I have yet to hear from some, and that surprised me.

At the same time, there were others—friends and acquaintances—who continued to reach out. And there were all those people waiting patiently at the grave in below-zero temperatures.

I have asked different friends about this and the response is often: "Well, some people have a hard time with death."

I don't have a great deal of sympathy for someone who can't do the right thing because they "have a hard time with death." That answer just doesn't cut it. Death *is* hard. There is no easy way to deal with it, but isn't that what adults are supposed to do—deal with difficult matters?

Rightly or wrongly, I have measured people by how they reacted to Lisa's illness and death.

I will also add that I need to take my own advice, because I have not always been true to my word.

I keep trying to do better.

I want to be more like Mary Kresky.

CHAPTER 17

Mary Kresky

FOUR YEARS AFTER LISA DIED, I was reading the obits in the paper and came across the name, Mary Kresky. It was familiar, but I couldn't place her. Only after checking my email log, I remembered the correspondence I had with her.

Mary Kresky called and visited Lisa when she was sick. Often, when I came home from work, I would hear that Mary Kresky had been by. Mary attended Lisa's funeral and came to the Shiva at our home. We spoke briefly afterwards, and we tried to get together for coffee, but, as things often go, she was busy or I was, and then we lost track of each other. This was my loss.

To honor Mary for her kindness and caring, I attended her funeral mass at a beautiful, small Catholic church near Columbia University, Corpus Christi. What I learned from the service was the caring, decent person that I came to know *was* Mary Kresky. People told many stories of this incredibly generous, kind, and thoughtful human being. Even though she had held powerful positions in state government, she always made time for other people. She always did the right thing.

I was astounded when, at the beginning of the Mass, Father Leo O'Donovan introduced two of Mary's nieces who recited the Jewish Kaddish prayer in English *and* Hebrew. At first, I thought I was hallucinating. That had to be the first time Kaddish was recited in Corpus Christi. I later learned that was something Mary had requested in honor of her late husband who was Jewish.

Father O'Donovan explained that he grew up in that church with Mary and her brother. Corpus Christi seemed to instill the right values and I came away from the mass and the entire experience with one lesson: "Be more like Mary Kresky."

A week later and just 20 blocks south of the church, I spent the day in our synagogue for Yom Kippur services with Claire. Our rabbi, Jeremy Kalmanovsky, gave a beautiful sermon that was, on one level, so simple, and on another, so needed at this particular time in our world: "Try to be a better human being."

When the Rabbi finished, I turned to Claire and whispered, "Be more like Mary Kresky."

I don't always succeed…but I keep trying.

CHAPTER 18

A Nice Woman

I SPENT THAT FIRST SUMMER after Lisa died at our family home in Wisconsin and I found myself going to the cemetery often. I felt the need to be near her, and another part of me didn't want her to be alone. She was so sensitive about that during her illness.

The Hensler family lives down the road in an old farmhouse. They watch our place when we are not there. The Henslers are devout Christians and just about the most wonderful people you will ever meet.

Mrs. Hensler notices things. She noticed I was losing weight and one day, I found a container of baked cookies she left in my kitchen. (Lisa's death seemed to open the cookie spigot.) She also noticed that I was going to the cemetery a lot.

One day when we were talking, she shared something her pastor once said about cemeteries: "It's a place to visit... not a place to stay."

Those words had a profound impact on me. I realized that what she was telling me was actually very Jewish. We are not supposed to go into the grave with departed loved ones. Life is the most valued gift a human being receives from God. I have always marveled how the survivors of the Holocaust walked out of those horrific nightmares and never sought revenge. Instead, they were focused only on rebuilding their lives, making new families, having children, in some cases, after losing children. They chose life. I had to as well.

I also realized that I was not setting a good example for my daughter. I stopped going to the grave so often.

Mrs. Hensler is a very kind woman. She notices things.

CHAPTER 19

A Not Nice Woman

ABOUT A YEAR AFTER LISA died, I finally went through her computer. I had been avoiding it. A person's computer is very intimate. There were photos of us I hadn't seen. Lovely emails between us that I had forgotten. It was a look at our days together from a slightly different angle. There were a lot of work-related items and a great deal of research on her illness. Lisa was a very smart clinician, and she probably knew as much about her cancer as the doctors treating her, which explains why she questioned them constantly. They treated her with great respect, but I think she had to be a difficult patient at times.

There were a lot of medical announcements from various organizations, theater ticket offerings and sale offers from Saks and Bergdorf (boy, did they ever lose a good customer). But going further back, I noticed old emails from two college girl friends that I knew she had fallen out of touch with.

I never heard from either, so I assumed they didn't know she'd died. I sent them each a first email from my computer, asking if this address still worked for them.

Both responded quickly and the first added that she was surprised to hear from me and hoped that Lisa, Claire, and I were doing well.

I sent her a second email explaining that I knew it had been a long time, that she and Lisa had fallen out of touch, and I was very sorry to have to tell her that Lisa got sick and died a year ago.

That first friend wrote back almost immediately, saying she was in shock, she was so sorry for Claire and for me, and she would spend the rest of her life upset that she fell out of touch with Lisa. It was truly heartfelt.

I sent the same email—word for word—to the second person and all I got back was stone silence. Not even "I'm sorry." I've always wondered what that was about. There was a bit of history here. She and Lisa were friends from college and had restarted the friendship here in New York. We often got together with her and her husband socially and invited them to all of our family events. But in that first summer after Lisa was diagnosed, she was hospitalized. Lisa reached out to this friend and the response was that she was at her vacation house for the month of August and couldn't come into the city from Connecticut. I was appalled and asked Lisa what she thought.

"Well," Lisa said matter-of-factly, "I guess she isn't the friend I thought she was."

In retrospect, the stone-cold response to my email was consistent.

But it made me also think about Emily Post and how our world has become so devoid of the basic manners that make living in it a more respectful, kinder, and more gracious place to live.

CHAPTER 20

How to Comport Yourself at a Funeral

IN HER BOOK *THE YEAR of Magical Thinking*, Joan Didion references (and resurrects) Emily Post's 1922 book on etiquette. I have always been fascinated with Emily Post. Besides teaching several generations of Americans which fork to use at dinner and what to say when you meet your future mother-in-law, Mrs. Post's book became the benchmark for how we should behave and, especially given today's breakdown in decorum, she made our country a better place to reside.

Mrs. Post was also very popular with the large wave of immigrants who came to the US at the turn of the 20th Century. She was an upper-class Manhattan doyenne who grew up in the Victorian era. My take on her writings a century later is that there is great wisdom in these pages. For instance, in Chapter XXIV, Mrs. Post tells Americans how to conduct themselves at a funeral:

Enter the church as quietly as possible, and as there are no ushers at a funeral, seat yourself where you approximately belong. Only a very intimate friend should take a position far up on the center aisle. If you are merely an acquaintance you should sit inconspicuously in the rear somewhere, unless the funeral is very small and the church big, in which case you may sit on the end seat of the center aisle toward the back.[8]

Emily Post goes on to suggest a friend stay behind at the home during the funeral service to help put things in order for the return of the mourners. She suggests warm broth or hot tea when they arrive: "…and it should be brought to them upon their return without their being asked if they would care for it. Those who are in great distress want no food, but if it is handed to them, they will mechanically take it, and something warm to start digestion and stimulate impaired circulation is what they most need."[9]

Emily Post is on the mark, but it also bespeaks of a very different world when, as Joan Didion pointed out, "mourning was still recognized, allowed, not hidden from view."[10]

I am reminded of a story my father once told me. He came home from college when his grandfather passed

---

8   Joan Didion, *The Year of Magical Thinking*, p. 58. Random House, 2005.

9   Ibid, p. 59.

10   Ibid, p. 59.

away. This would have been in the 1930s. He said it was an orthodox Jewish funeral and it was in the home. I was horrified, thinking of having a casket and a dead body in my home. In retrospect and after so many years, that intimacy with death struck me as wiser than the sanitized version that has developed since. That old way, I believe, brought a greater understanding and acceptance of death and would, ultimately, make it less frightening, not more.

This is where Didion hits the mark pitch perfect:

Philippe Aries, in a series of lectures he delivered at Johns Hopkins in 1973 and later published as *Western Attitudes towards Death: From the Middle Ages to the Present*, noted that beginning about 1930 there had been in most Western countries and particularly in the United States a revolution in accepted attitudes toward death. "Death," he wrote, "so omnipresent in the past that it was familiar, would be effaced, would disappear. It would become shameful and forbidden."[11]

My memory of the shiva was of playing host. Making sure I spent the proper amount of time with everyone, thanking them for coming and asking them if they would like something to eat or drink. Even though this is *not* the way a shiva is supposed to work, it helped me practice

11   Joan Didion, *The Year of Magical Thinking*, p.60. Random House, 2005.

being normal at an abnormal time. In orthodox homes, the bereaved sit on special low chairs that are close to the floor and they stay there. Visitors come to them and express their condolences. Like Emily Post suggests, the bereaved are brought food.

The mourners stay inside the house for a week. They don't go out. When the shiva ends after one week, they go outside and walk around the block. This is more than symbolic. Those first footsteps in the outside air signal the beginning of their new lives.

I went out…mostly to a small orthodox synagogue or "shtible" in the neighborhood. The regulars are an incredibly kind and thoughtful group. They have been tremendously supportive to me throughout it all.

I went most mornings for the traditional eleven months of mourning to recite Kaddish. The rabbi there keeps track of all the members. When my period of mourning ended, he walked directly over to me at the end of the services and said succinctly, but with care:

"Your mourning period is over. Get up! And may all go well with you and your daughter in the future."

The "Get up!" sounded like a command and in a way it was, but it was also a hope and it came from this kind man's heart. It was meant to set me off in the right direction through the rest of my life. To help me not wallow in my grief. To help me live. It was also one of the most challenging directives I have ever been given.

I will add one more memory.

I grew up in Milwaukee in the 1950s and 1960s. My parents did not go out that often, especially on weekday nights. When I noticed them leaving, I asked where they were going. Nine times out of ten, their answer: "We're *paying* a condolence call." That was the term they used, paying. I wonder if it was like banking—doing this because someday they would need to be "repaid."

Didion continues here:

In both England and the United States, Gorer observed, the contemporary trend was "to treat mourning as morbid self-indulgence, and to give social admiration to the bereaved who hide their grief so fully that no one would guess anything happened."

One way in which grief gets hidden is that death now occurs largely offstage. In the earlier tradition from which Mrs. Post wrote, the act of dying had not yet been professionalized. It did not typically involve hospitals. Women died in childbirth. Children died of fevers. Cancer was untreatable. At the time she undertook her book of etiquette, there would have been few American households untouched by the influenza pandemic of 1918. Death was up close, at home. The average adult was expected to deal competently, and also sensitively, with its aftermath.[12]

With little prior understanding of any of this, I had decided on my own to make Lisa's dying home-based. It just made the most sense to me. This might not work for others, but it worked for me and I am glad I did it this way.

---

12   Ibid.

CHAPTER 21

Spotify

MY DAUGHTER INTRODUCED ME TO Spotify sometime after Lisa's death and I have become one of its biggest fans. It's made my life happier at a time when I needed some happiness.

I now listen to it at home, at the gym, walking to work through Central Park, on airplanes and rowing on our lake in Wisconsin. The only time I don't listen to it is when I'm swimming.

For those of you who don't know the streaming service, you can choose practically any song ever recorded and hear it immediately—classical, rock, folk, jazz, *anything*. You make different playlists of whatever songs you are in the mood to hear. There is also an algorithm that follows what you are listening to and offers different musicians you might not know who are somewhat similar.

It was this algorithm that introduced me to what I thought were some amazingly talented Norwegian female singers. One day, after telling my next-door neighbor about them, she asked to hear them. She is from Copenhagen and when I played them for her, she looked at me like I was an idiot. They weren't Norwegian; they were Swedish. In my limited experience with Scandinavia, I didn't realize there was a difference in the language. Those lovely Swedish women (formerly Norwegian) gave me great comfort. I was also struck by the large number of absolutely beautiful songs that focus on loss. I never realized there were so many. I guess I never really listened to the words that closely. These songs can still move me to tears, but my God, they are beautiful.

Eva Cassidy will break your heart, but you won't be able to stop listening to her. Eva died of cancer at 33, virtually unknown. But two of her recordings were played on the BBC after her death and there was a huge response. Long after she was gone, millions of people came to love her. One of her songs was featured in one of my favorite films, *Love Actually*. But it's her rendition of "Fields of Gold" that brings Lisa back to me every single time. Thank you for that, Eva, and God bless you.

(I will include several of my playlists)

"I Saw a Stranger with Your Hair" by John Gorka

"I Waited for You" by Daniel Norgren

"Killing Me" by Luke Sital-Singh

"Once I Was Loved" by Melody Gardot

"If We Were Vampires" by Jason Isbell

"Song to the Siren" by Tim Buckley

"Shoreline" by Anna Ternheim

"Sand and Water" by Beth Nielsen Chapman

"Mind" by Sarah Klang

"Lost without You" by Freya Ridings

Last but not least, "I Know You by Heart" by Eva Cassidy. I dare you to listen to this with dry eyes.

…And so many more you wouldn't believe.

CHAPTER 22

No Surprise, Hollywood Doesn't Get It…at All

WHAT IS IT ABOUT THE alluring widower? What makes a man more appealing if his wife is dead? Is he more vulnerable? More available? He doesn't get any better looking… or smarter…or richer (unless his dead wife was an heiress). But Hollywood has leaned on this scenario from the start: the sad widower who everyone wants to help. It's also completely one-sided. I can't think of similar films where the widow allures.

Hollywood's somewhat distorted version of the widower makes complete box office sense. No one would pay money to see the reality. What normal person would want to spend two hours watching Brad Pitt or Robert Redford make coffee in the morning, sit down by himself, stare at his cup for ten minutes in silence and then burst into tears? (Well, maybe Ingmar Bergman fans.) Great entertainment and great dialogue don't include sleepless nights and hours of loneliness and longing.

Even Daniel Craig's first Bond film sets up his torment over the loss of his great love, Vesper, that carries through to every Bond film that follows. If the death of love can put an ever-so-slight dent in James Bond's armor, it can certainly make mincemeat of us mortals. (No criticism of Craig here, he was a terrific Bond.)

I have found most films on this topic fairly awful, embarrassing and even insulting. In 1963, we had the amazingly facile *The Courtship of Eddie's Father*, which actually went on to become a network comedy series for three seasons in the 1970s. Yes, you read that correctly— comedy. The 1963 film stars Glenn Ford as the recent widower, a network radio executive with a young son played by Ron Howard. No sooner does Ford return to work from the funeral that everyone, including his son, starts to help find him a new wife. Everyone gets involved. It feels like Ford lost his housekeeper—not anyone he was remotely attached to. He never loses his composure, he doesn't appear to be sad, and his son is the quintessential 1950s American kid, more interested in pretty much everything else except the fact that he's lost his mother.

This would fall into the category of *sanitizing* death.

More recent films like *Sleepless in Seattle* are slightly better. There is at least one honest scene when Tom Hanks gets exasperated with his young son, and the boy actually breaks down over the loss. But the immediate fall for Meg

Ryan with his adorable son pushing the idea is sweet but, at least for me, unrealistic.

Hanks gets closer on his second try, 20 years later, in *A Man Called Otto*. A sad, angry old man who wants nothing more than to kill himself and join his wife. I saw aspects of myself in the grumpy old man part and the movie reminded me to tone it down.

Love Actually used the same tact with Liam Neeson as the widower who looks like he is truly in great pain and actually loved the wife he lost…until he moves on with the promise of supermodel Claudia Shiffer. Who can say no to a supermodel?

However, there is one brief moment where the film industry caught the truth of what it means to lose your spouse and, strangely, it seems almost by accident. Perhaps that's because widowhood isn't the main point of *To Kill a Mockingbird*. It is, of course, about race in the 1930s South. But Gregory Peck, as Atticus Finch, is completely believable as a widower when he is just sitting outside on the porch by himself one summer night. His two young children are in their bedrooms about to fall asleep, and Atticus overhears a conversation between them concerning their dead mother. Scout asks her brother if he remembers her because her memory is fading. What makes this scene so incredibly powerful is the fact that Gregory Peck says absolutely nothing. He has no lines. While we also eavesdrop on the children's conversation, the camera just focuses on Atticus as he sits there, taking it in…alone. It's all in his face. This scene is thoughtful, respectful, and as powerful as any I have ever seen.

A friend suggested I watch a series on Netflix called *Afterlife* by British comedian Ricky Gervais. It's about a British reporter for a local small-town paper in England who has lost his wife. The deceased wife appears throughout the series in video recordings that he watches most nights.

It was touching and, in many ways, so accurate that I felt very sorry for Gervais. I just assumed that his keen understanding of the topic must have come from actual experience. I was greatly relieved and frankly surprised to look him up and see he is not, in real life, a widower. I am curious, though, how he got it so right. I think he's a very insightful and talented man.

One night, I rewatched *The American President* with Michael Douglas, which was the genesis for the later series, *The West Wing*. Douglas plays a widower president with a teenage daughter, and he starts dating a high-powered lobbyist played by Annette Bening. It hurt so much not because of the movie, but because I first saw it with Lisa. Now, all these years later, there I was watching it alone, never imagining that I would be in his shoes. (Obviously not the White House part, nor Annette Bening.)

But the all-time *Blech* Award goes to the insipid, cliché-filled, and horribly acted 1970 film *Love Story* with Ali McGraw and Ryan O'Neal. The story, which was extremely popular when it came out, uses the heroine's cancer as a vehicle for tear-jerk sympathy. Here it is again, the vulnerable, appealing widower. (I remember hearing loud sobs in the theater when I saw it in my freshman year of college, followed by laughter from a crowd of cynical students.).

I watched it again recently to make sure my memory was correct. Now, 50 years later, it's even *worse* than I remembered. Actually, I really don't know what was worse—the story itself, the clichéd script, or the acting. Probably all three. This is a film that can make you vomit.

It worked though—at least financially. *Love Story* was one of the first films to make $100 million in its initial run. That was a lot of money in 1970. The book by Erich Segal was on the best seller list for 41 weeks.

I found absolutely nothing romantic in my wife's cancer, the long days and nights in the hospital, her suffering or her death. Zilch. (I do remember the compassion of the night nurses at the desk when I would leave around midnight. It was always in their faces as I walked out.)

By the way, my favorite part of the *Love Story* story is that Segal's book was nominated for the National Book Award, but then withdrawn when the judges, God bless them, threatened to resign.

Finally, I have my own video library that I must be so careful with because I could spend all of my evenings watching it. There are long videos of Lisa reading to Claire from the age of three months on or dancing with her around the apartment. She did this every night when she came home from work to Claire's delight. Actually, to the delight of all three of us.

I have wondered how this new technology changes our relationship with the dead. Since the beginning of time until very recently, human beings did not have the ability to see any image of their departed loved ones, much less hear their voices. Photography began only in the 19th century and became available to everyone later in the 20th. Even in my childhood, Super 8 film had no sound. Now, there is no need to thread a projector. My computer is filled with videos and conversations with Lisa, available anytime at the touch of a finger. I see her; I hear her; I know her smile, her words, her laugh. She is as alive again as ever.

These videos don't make me sad. I feel connected to her again when I see them, but I wonder if not having this access to her would help me move on faster.

There is one video that always mesmerizes me. It captures the happiest moment of my life. We are standing under our chuppah, I have just broken the glass and kissed the bride, our friends and family in the synagogue burst into applause as the music strikes up. Everyone in the synagogue is clapping as we turn towards them with the widest smiles you've ever seen on two people, and we walk back up the aisle clasping hands, now as husband and wife.

But here is the moment that gets me every time. As we leave the sanctuary and walk out the door into the empty hallway beyond, the camera stays on us and catches us as we turn toward each other and kiss one more time before we turn to the left and disappear into the blinding noontime light streaming in through the windows. The glare from the sunlight takes over the entire frame.

There goes Lisa, disappearing on me again.

CHAPTER 23

The Paperwork of Death

As if a death weren't bad enough, the government will also intrude and not in a helpful manner. Both federal and state (some states are greedier than others) will want a portion of anything the deceased leaves behind and you will have to deal with it. Putting this together will take hours of work and it's complicated, but not impossible.

I was methodical with all the paperwork surrounding Lisa's death. As I went through the tasks, I chronicled everything in a blue binder with tabs. In some ways, this was actually cathartic in that it gave me something to do that I could actually concentrate on—a distraction if you will. There is a certainty with numbers, unlike almost everything else.

The work included:

- Closing all her accounts.

- Notifying various banks and brokerage companies.

- Closing her credit cards.

- Notifying Social Security.

- I had to hire an attorney to go through probate because I stupidly overlooked something basic, which I will explain.

- Eventually, I would have to cancel her cell phone, but I waited on that. Strangely, I didn't want it turned off. Maybe I was hoping for a call from her. (Talk about long distance.)

- Dealing with the insurance companies.

- And, notifying her employer that she died and cleaning out her office (which was heartbreaking).

We had each maintained separate checking accounts. I took care of all the household bills with my account. She took care of her personal expenses on her account. I think the biggest reason for the separate accounts --she didn't want me to know the cost of getting her hair colored or how much she spent at Bergdorf's, which she kept from me. She was correct.

We held all of our investments together in one account. That wasn't the problem. But for the smaller ones, we never named each other as beneficiaries. I assumed, wrongly, that our wills would have sufficed. Hence, probate.

There were also hospital bills, which I paid immediately, as is my wont. Big mistake. The bills were wrong on their end, and it took dozens more calls, over and over, to try to get a refund, which they owed me. My guess is that they have a policy of waiting you out. Eventually, a lot of people just give up or forget and the hospital (or insurance company) pockets the money. I'm sure it adds up.

Lisa handled all the medical insurance since she was a physician. I didn't realize that we had met our deductible and these bills were sent in error. In one case, I had to make 50 calls over a period of months to get a refund on $50.00. I'm sure it wasn't worth my time, but it was the principle. I spoke to the same lady on the phone every time who admitted that it was their error, but she told me that the bill had to be "reviewed" by various committees. Again, I am convinced that this is done on purpose because people will eventually let it go. I'm sure an actuary has figured out the percentage of these bills that eventually becomes cash for them. There is also a great deal of incompetence. I dealt with people on the other end of the phone who didn't always know what they were doing.

Social Security is no different. Lisa had her wages deducted since her first job at Roy Rogers when she was 17. She died before she took out a dime. I received a small benefit from it, but just for a brief time until my own account kicked in. Interestingly, the Social Security people that I dealt with were among the most helpful and kind.

One day, I finally got so fed up with it all—especially the hospitals and insurance companies—that I wrote an op-ed in the *Wall Street Journal* on my experience. Then, something strange happened. Before it was to be published, I desperately needed the *WSJ* to add a picture of Lisa. The editors graciously agreed, and it meant so much that her photo appeared in the paper with over a million subscribers. I needed her not to be forgotten.

Online readers can offer their own opinions on every *Wall Street Journal* op-ed and this particular article received more comments than many of my political pieces. I realize this may sound silly, but the most gratifying were those that talked about the photo—how beautiful she was.

Two comments stood out for me.

A man named Robert Shulz wrote, "Amazing how the emotional impact of a story is increased when a picture is provided."

To which Charleen Larson responded, "Honestly? It gutted me."

Eventually, the bills were paid, the estate was closed, I paid her last charges, and her accounting with the government was complete. Washington and Albany would finally let her rest in peace.

I put her dead cell phone along with her wallet in the top drawer of my desk, where they both still sit. All the papers fill three files in a small white cabinet in a closet. They sit next to the estate files of my parents and my grandfather—along with tax returns, bills, and some letters that I found meaningful. Eventually, they will all be tossed out by descendants who never met their grandmother or great-grandparents.

This is the way we all will eventually disappear.

From the *Wall Street Journal*, April 27, 2018:

YOU CAN LIMIT DEATH'S FINANCIAL COSTS, IF NOT THE EMOTIONAL ONES

By Warren Kozak
April 27, 2018 6:34 pm ET

The transfer of assets when a spouse dies can be fairly simple—if you learn from my mistakes.

The author's late wife, Dr. Lisa Jane Krenzel.

I pride myself on keeping meticulous financial records. But since my wife died on Jan. 1, I discovered I had made some real rookie mistakes that led to hours of extra work and substantial fees. The transfer of assets between spouses can be fairly simple—if you learn from my mistakes.

Dr. Lisa Jane Krenzel and I shared everything throughout our marriage. Like many couples, we split responsibilities. I paid the bills and made investments. She took care of our health insurance, plus the house. We maintained individual checking and savings accounts, as well as separate retirement accounts from various jobs throughout our careers. What went wrong?

Issue One: When we opened those checking and savings accounts, we never named beneficiaries. I had assumed, incorrectly, that our accounts would simply transfer to the other in case of death. The banker who opened the accounts never suggested otherwise. With a named beneficiary, her accounts would have simply been folded into mine. Instead, I had to hire a lawyer— at $465 an hour—to petition the court to name me as the executor of her estate. I needed this power to transfer her accounts. Filing costs in New York City for the necessary document was $1,286. The running bill for the lawyer stands at $7,402.00, and I expect it to rise.

I also needed the documents for the companies that managed her retirement accounts and a mutual fund, because, as at the bank, we never named a beneficiary.

By the way, this paperwork also required signature guarantees or a notary seal, which can take up an afternoon.

Issue Two: The highly charged question of funeral and burial. Last summer, when I was told Lisa would not survive this illness, I tried to raise the issue of burial with her. She refused to have the conversation, but I quietly went ahead and purchased a plot of graves in the cemetery in Wisconsin where my parents, grandparents, and great-grandparents are buried. This was something I actually did right.

We had to employ two funeral homes—one in New York and one in Wisconsin—and her body had to make the journey out there. All told, I spent $46,359 to cover funeral expenses, graves, transportation, a headstone, and a basic casket.

I noticed something interesting in this process. All of my fellow baby boomer friends I have since asked have so far refused to deal with the issue. They wince when I even raise the question. Hear me: You don't want to have to make this decision at the time someone close to you dies. You simply are not thinking straight.

Issue Three: Our health insurance plan covered the long hospital stays and doctors' visits. However, shortly after Lisa died, I still received bills, even though our deductibles and copays had long since been covered.

I paid them immediately, which was a mistake. I was incorrectly billed and I have been fighting the hospitals and insurance company since January to get a refund, even though everyone agrees the bills were incorrect. Before you pay any medical bills, make a simple call and determine their legitimacy. Mistakes are constant: the systems are so complicated, even people in these offices don't always understand the intricacies.

Issue Four: Lisa had two life-insurance policies—one through her work and the other we purchased privately. The former was handled quickly and efficiently by her job and a check arrived almost immediately. Although the insurance company sent me a check for her private policy soon after her death, it took three months of constant calls and emails to determine a refund of the premium I had already paid for three months past her death. I kept getting wrong information from the company, because the people I dealt with didn't understand it themselves.

Issue Five: Over the course of Lisa's working life—from her first job at a fast-food restaurant to medicine—she paid more than $100,000 to Social Security. Since she died at 60, and our 19-year-old daughter is one year past the age of receiving a monthly benefit, all this money has simply disappeared into the lockbox in Washington. Nothing you can do about this one.

Finally, there is the major psychological trauma of grief. I think most people believe death will never intrude on their lives and when it does, we will be so old and decrepit that it won't much matter. Trust me on this— even when it's been expected for a while, it still shocks deeply. There is absolutely no way you can prepare yourself for the shattering heartbreak of loss. When it did come to me, I found the support of friends, family, and faith to be invaluable. Amazingly, that cost nothing.

CHAPTER 24

Check List

THIS HAS NOTHING TO DO with grief, but it has everything to do with making your spouse's or children's lives easier after you die. You can ease their trauma by preparing a lot of the work in advance and making this period for them at least a little less complicated.

Here is a list of a few things that will certainly help. You should also seek further advice from a lawyer and a financial expert.

1. Have an up-to-date will. (This is so basic, but a high percentage of people put this off and wind up dying without one. Don't be one of these people.)

2. Name your wife/husband/child as your chief beneficiary on *every* single financial document. Every single one!

3. If there are no immediate relatives, find an organization(s) you respect and leave the money to them.

4. Decide where and how you want to be buried or cremated.

5. If you decide on burial, buy the plot of graves now (you'll save money since the price will only go up and it will save your relatives from having to make a big decision at a time when it's hard to make *any* decisions).

6. Write out instructions that address the following:

7. List where all of your assets are located (which banks, brokerage houses, etc.).

8. Put down your passwords so your survivors can get into your computer and view these accounts.

9. Put these instructions in a file, followed by a copy of your will in the second file, followed by a file with all important documents, insurance policies, deeds, or proof of ownership to home, car, or anything else of value. Tell someone you trust where this all is.

10. I have a friend who has even suggested writing your own obituary. Who knows you better? I have not done this, but you may want to try it.

11. Leave instructions for your funeral, including where you want it held and who you want to speak.

12. Update this instruction document every six months or at least once a year and print an additional copy and give it to the person you have named as executor of your estate.

13. Regarding personal possessions, you may want to name who gets which items.

Some people may think this is all morbid. It's not. It's inevitable. You are just making the lives of your loved ones easier. You are being the adult.

CHAPTER 25

A Great Question

A LITTLE OVER A YEAR after Lisa died, Claire and I traveled to San Francisco for the wedding of one of her favorite cousins. Afterwards, I had to be in Israel for work and she had to be in London for a college program a week later. So I suggested she fly with me to Tel Aviv, and after my work was finished, we could travel together for a few days. Then she would go off to London and I would fly home.

One night, while we were having dinner in a lovely restaurant, we talked. I mean really talked. No time crunch. No place we needed to go. Out of the blue, she asked me the most intriguing question that I later turned into another *Wall Street Journal* column. It was a very short piece, but it received the most reaction from any of my columns.

DAD, DID YOU ACHIEVE ALL YOUR LIFE GOALS?

My daughter's question showed me my aims at 21 weren't what they are now.

By Warren Kozak
Aug. 2, 2019

I don't often get a question that stops me in my tracks. But on a recent vacation, my daughter and I had the rare opportunity to sit down and talk in a relaxed setting. We're at very different stages in our lives. She is 21, going into her senior year of college with the whole world in front of her. I'm 68—most of my friends are retiring.

She turned to me at dinner and asked if I had met the goals I set for myself when I was her age. What an interesting question, I thought. First, I tried to remember what I thought I even wanted nearly half a century ago and then summon the honesty to measure some sort of success ratio.

The first part took some doing. I do remember seeing everything in those days through a professional lens. What kind of job would I have? How much money would I make? Might I even become "famous"? (I'm not at all sure how I defined fame back then.)

After sleeping on it, I told her the next morning that I was surprised to find what I consider my greatest accomplishments today are not even remotely close to what I might have imagined back then.

None of my professional achievements are anywhere near the top of the list, and that shocked me.

What I am most proud of, I told her, was standing by her mother through a long illness that eventually took her life—being a faithful husband, and, I hope, a good father. I am proud to say I consider myself a loyal friend, I've lived an honest life (at least since high school), and I never disgraced my parents or my country.

Never, in a million years, would I have expected to be saying any of this when I was her age. It was everything I learned in religious school, the Boy Scouts, and the Milwaukee public-school system of the 1950s and '60s. Perhaps most astonishing, it was even part of the little morality lessons that I saw on TV shows, like *Leave It to Beaver* and *Father Knows Best*. Television has changed a lot since my childhood, and not for the better.

The Ten Commandments are not part of the curriculum in public schools anymore, and that's a shame. I have great pride in having violated them as infrequently as possible.

But I advised her that I am still a work in progress and could mess up royally before it's all over. I added that it's a great question, but you have to grow into the answer.

CHAPTER 26

Burial

ONE OF THE TOPICS I touched on in the first op-ed was burial. As I said earlier, Lisa could not deal with her impending death. It was one of her greatest fears. She lost her mother when she was 12 years old and the idea that she would leave her daughter as she was left was too much for her.

There were, however, brief moments when she would address it. She knew I wanted to be buried at the cemetery in Wisconsin near the graves of my family. And we both expressed our revulsion with her family's cemetery in Philadelphia, which was rundown, poorly maintained, and just about the last place in the world anyone would want to remain for eternity.

Once, during one of those long days in the hospital, when she was in bed trying to read or watch something on her iPad and I was sitting next to her working on my computer, she just said: "I guess I'll be buried in Wisconsin."

I said nothing, just acknowledged that I heard her. She also said she didn't want a service in a funeral home. I suggested our synagogue and she seemed to agree, but she wondered if the rabbi knew her well enough. I told her I would speak. This would be the most consequential talk we had about her impending death.

I would always answer these queries by talking about what I wanted for myself. After a long pause, I said that I would want an orthodox funeral, which means a plain pine box, no embalming, closed casket. She said that would be ok, but she didn't want to be resting on a hard wood surface. I told her I would make sure she wasn't, and she isn't. She would rest on a bed of what looked like hay or straw.

This conversation gave me "permission" to move ahead and make some of the arrangements. Sometime later, when I had to be in Wisconsin, I went to the cemetery and walked around with the manager. Our family plot would not accommodate all of the next generation, so I bought a plot of eight graves in a new field that had just opened. It sits under the shade of a tree. There were no other graves in the new field yet. Hers would be the first (and strangely, it remains so five years later).

When she died, I was relieved to have one less item to decide.

Amazingly, so many people avoid doing this. Granted, it's not an uplifting topic, but it's necessary and inevitable. Once again, it will help those left behind.

CHAPTER 27

One Last Goodbye

BECAUSE LISA WAS BURIED IN that new field, I had to purchase a new headstone. My family plot has one large headstone that just reads "KOZAK," and then each individual has smaller stones with their name, the dates, and the same in Hebrew.

The first decision was what to put on the large stone. Should it be just Kozak? Or should I add Krenzel to it, which was her family name and the one she used? I asked various relatives, but the person whose opinion carried the most weight was Claire. She didn't hesitate for a moment.

"Just Kozak," she said. "Time to bring her into the fold."

In truth, near the end of her life, one of those little comments that Lisa said out of the blue, that really surprised me, touched on this. "I should have changed my name," she said one day. "We should all have had the same name."

I always wished she had but respected her reasoning for not doing this. All of her medical licenses would have to be changed and everyone already knew her professionally as Dr. Krenzel. But I think everyone in a family should have the same name and I was gratified that she came to this conclusion as well.

It was around that time that Lisa was weighing her life and the choices she had made on several fronts. She also said one afternoon that one of the best decisions she ever made was letting her career stall, so she could spend more time with Claire as she grew up. She never regretted that.

So the new gravestone would just say "KOZAK."

I came to know the two maintenance workers at the cemetery, because I was there a lot; both very nice guys. Before the headstone was set down, I learned they had to dig a large hole and pour in a bed of concrete as a base for it to rest on. Otherwise, the stone would soon sink into the ground from its weight and tilt.

I asked them to call me when they did this. I wanted to be there, although I really didn't know what to expect. I think this was a vestige of being with her through all the hospital stays. Maybe it was one last way to protect her – from what, I don't know.

It turns out, they literally dug up the grave right down to the coffin. When they were done, there was a large open area and the top third of the casket was plainly visible, right there in front of me. I was surprised how badly it had deteriorated already; it was only about five months. Then again, I had never seen a buried casket.

Without asking—and I couldn't believe I was doing this, but it was almost involuntary—I put my hands along the sides of the open grave and lowered myself down into it. I knelt next to the casket and rested my hand on the top of it for a long while. Without saying anything, the guys understood and turned around and walked away for a time, giving me some privacy. I never expected to be that close to her again and it gave me tremendous comfort and even happiness. I imagined Lisa lifting her hand on the inside and reaching out to touch mine.

What an unexpected gift.

CHAPTER 28

A Higher Authority

RELIGION HAS BECOME SUCH A charged topic today. I mentioned this earlier. If my own friends are a microcosm of the general population, they span the entire spectrum. Some are devout believers in God, others not at all. Some attend weekly and even daily services, some haven't set foot in a church or synagogue in years.

I have never sought to proselytize. As I stated in the beginning, I believe one's religious beliefs, like their political beliefs, are their own business. But, let's be honest, how can you even begin to talk about death without mentioning religion? The two are inevitably intertwined. I've always thought that one of the reasons for the development of religions in the first place, thousands of years ago, was to help human beings *deal* with death. To give us guidance, structure, understanding, hope.

So, I offer my own personal thoughts on religion now and how all of this related to the death of my wife with the complete understanding that some readers will disagree. I have no problem with that. In fact, if it's an issue you feel strongly about one way or the other, jump now to the next chapter. No offense taken.

Throughout Lisa's illness and after her death, I found my beliefs were altered in a way I didn't expect. The disease had a profound effect on Lisa as well. During her illness, Lisa's attachment to religion and God grew stronger. This could easily be explained by the "no atheists in foxholes" theory.

We used to joke that we had a *mixed* marriage. Although both of us were Jewish, my belief was stronger. Hers less so. But as the illness progressed, she became more devout. She prayed more. She asked me to join her reciting prayers every night. She met often with our rabbi and a good friend who is a rabbi. Another friend arranged a meeting with a very important Rebbe[13] who was visiting from Israel and gave her a blessing. I have watched Catholics ask the Pope for similar blessings. It is altogether human to reach out to those rare individuals whom we believe to have a closer connection to God than the rest of us.

Lisa's silent prayers, I assumed, asked God to restore her health and allow her to live. Those prayers were not answered, at least not in the way she hoped. But, after

---

13   A spiritual leader in the Hasidic community, often with thousands of followers. Rebbes are highly intelligent, very learned, and wise. Some are believed to have extraordinary powers of thought. The leadership of each dynasty is passed down through the first-born son.

watching her suffer and die, to my great surprise, my own belief in God grew even stronger. I think I can deconstruct this, but forgive me, I need to say this one last time: this worked for me and may not work for you.

Let me summarize the strengthening of my beliefs this way: after all the stupid mistakes I made throughout my life, all the relationships that did not work, the entire panoply of wrong choices, missed opportunities, bad timing… the long journey on *the highway of regret*, I don't think my meeting Lisa was just some random accident of the universe, a happenstance, a coincidence.

We were born and raised in different states—Pennsylvania and Wisconsin—and we went to different colleges, studied different fields, worked in completely different professions, and even spent our free time very differently (she was active in a music and dance scene with just about the dorkiest people I have ever encountered in my life). Given all that, we happened to have just one friend in common, who actually went to the bother of inviting us both for dinner with the express purpose of having us meet. By the way, where did I meet our common friend?

In my synagogue.

I had a very close relationship with a brilliant Hasidic rabbi who once told me that all chuppahs (marriages) are announced in heaven. That they are all divinely inspired. Many Christians believe this as well. When Rabbi Chaskel

Besser told me this, I questioned him and brought up the fact that the divorce rate was over 50 percent today.

Without missing a beat, the Rabbi responded, "I said all chuppahs are *announced* in heaven. That doesn't mean everyone is listening."

I believe in my bones that Lisa and I were meant to be together. I believe our marriage, our chuppah, was, indeed, announced in heaven. In the end, because I am so grateful for having had her in my life, my thanks and belief in God grew stronger, in spite of the ending.

I know others who have gone through similar or worse traumas have taken a different direction. I've always been fascinated with the divergent reactions of survivors of the Holocaust. After seeing their entire families murdered, sometimes even their spouses and children, some became devout atheists. Some devout believers. Some became more Jewish, others completely abandoned Judaism. Not having gone through this nightmare, I wouldn't question either.

Rabbi Besser understood that not everyone believes in God. Everyone has free will to make this choice. If there were no free will, he said, then belief in God would be meaningless. We all have the choice to believe or not to believe. He once said that he felt truly sorry for non-religious people because life is just a lot easier to go through its traumas with a strong belief.

A woman named Carolyn Jones, whom I do not know and is clearly of another faith, echoed the Rabbi's thoughts in the comments section of the *Wall Street Journal* regarding the op-ed I wrote after Lisa's death. Ms. Jones wrote: "And that is the thing that will sustain one night after night, month after month, on into years. I despair for those without the outpouring of support when someone is literally at the foot of the Cross with grief. It has to be the loneliest journey in life."

In every Jewish prayer service, there is a silent prayer called the Amidah. That's when the service, which is always communal and may appear to outsiders to be more chaotic than a formal religious service in, say, a Protestant church, abruptly changes. It's the only time there is total silence in the room. The entire congregation stands and each person prays silently for several minutes. After Lisa died, the Amidah became the most important part of the service for me. It was the part I waited for. It was when I spoke to her.

As soon as the room quieted down, I imagined the sound we used to hear when we dropped a dime in a pay phone (younger readers will not know this sound and that's a shame). As soon as the coin was inserted and the line was established, I would start my conversation with her. I did this every morning. I would tell her all sorts of things: what I was thinking, how grateful I was that she was in my life, how much I loved her, and, of course, how much I missed her. There were also mornings when I was pissed off at her for various things that happened in the past and I told her so. (It was a marriage, after all.)

This was my time to really connect with her. I would ask for guidance with Claire. To watch over us. To guide and help Claire. I thanked God for putting Lisa in my life and giving me Claire.

When I mentioned these conversations to my therapist, he asked a reasonable question.

"Does she ever answer back?"

"Nope." I responded. "It's a very one-sided conversation."

But it gives me a sense of comfort.

Unlike C. S. Lewis and Rabbi Harold Kushner, who wrote the popular book, *When Bad Things Happen to Good People*, I found no need to wrestle with God over my loss. For me, it ultimately came down to this question: knowing that life is finite, that every marriage, every relationship, every life will end in death (if the marriage doesn't detonate sooner in divorce), how could I complain after receiving this fabulous gift in the first place?

That would be as ungrateful as it is arrogant.

But there is one more vital part to this story that gives me the courage to go forward. I am absolutely convinced that I will see Lisa again. And that keeps me going with an internal sense of contentment.

I have no idea the realm, the context, or the place. No idea how this will manifest itself. But I am sure that I will recognize her immediately and she will know me. I am just so sure of this.

CHAPTER 29

Going Home

On December 15, 2017, the hospice doctor and social worker at the hospital came to me and we spoke outside Lisa's room. They explained that there was nothing more that could be done in the hospital, and, in the most benign language possible of an impending death, they told me, "We were now at the stage where the only option is to make her as comfortable as possible."

They predicted (quite accurately, it turns out), that Lisa would die in a matter of days, maybe weeks, but not months. (It would be a little over two weeks— 16 days.) Even though I clearly heard what they were saying, I still could not accept it. I didn't really believe them.

They gave me two options. Lisa could be transferred to a hospice hospital in the Bronx called Calvary or I could bring her home.

I was already sure of my choice, but I went to see Calvary that afternoon anyway. The employees were warm and supportive and the facility, considering its purpose, was bright; everyone there struck me as cheerful and caring. Nice people, all.

My decision even before that hallway conversation with the palliative people was that I would bring Lisa home. Her final days would be in the home that we made together, the home where we raised our daughter, the home where we were a family. This was what I would have wanted if the tables were turned. And we *all* had had enough hospitals.

An ambulance brought her home. She first sat down in a comfortable chair in the living room, looking out at the Hudson River. How much she understood at that point, I don't know. But I could see in her face that she was happy to be in her own home, in her chair, surrounded by all the little things that were an important part of her life. Perhaps she never thought she would be back here again.

Over the next 16 days, she spent more and more time in bed. When she was able to sit with us at the dinner table, this highly intelligent woman was not always coherent. We could see that she could not follow the conversation, but it was also clear that she was happy being there with us.

Claire and I spent time with her in the bedroom, hugging her, telling her how much we loved her. I am not sure if any of this registered.

I have two strong memories of those final days, both so touching. One night, I heard Claire singing in our bedroom. She was sitting on the bed next to Lisa who was unconscious. Claire had found the lyrics on her phone for a girl scout campfire song that Lisa sang to her when she was a baby, "Barges."

It broke my heart to hear this and tears filled my eyes. I walked in to watch around the corner, and I saw Lisa lifting her arm in reaction to hearing the song. Even though she was not conscious, Claire's singing touched her on some fundamental level that I would never understand.

My other memory is this: one evening very near the end, Lisa wanted to come out and sit at the kitchen counter. I had to help her walk over. She didn't speak. She just wanted to sit there.

Our friend, Wing, with whom we would stay in Milwaukee in a matter of days for the burial, had sent us a special holiday gift—ten pints of ice cream from our favorite shop. I went to the freezer and took out the mint-chocolate chip—Lisa's favorite. At that point, she hadn't eaten anything for a couple of days. I knew how much she liked that ice cream and I gave her a teaspoon of it and put it in her mouth. She ate it and then motioned for another. She motioned one more time. I fed her three spoonfuls of her favorite ice cream. Those three spoonfuls of mint-chocolate chip would be the last thing she would ever eat.

Sixteen days after I brought her home from the hospital, Lisa took her last breath in our bed. She died in the home we made together, in the bed we shared. This was so incredibly appropriate to me.

I was there when the funeral people would come to pick her up. I would help place her on the stretcher and I would drive with her to the funeral home.

Some people may be repelled by being this close to death. I have never regretted my decision of bringing her back home. Not for a moment.

CHAPTER 30

Five Years On

WHAT HAVE I LEARNED FROM this death, which has, on one level, been so incredibly gut wrenching, so hard to fathom and on another, the greatest challenge and learning experience of my life?

First, there is good news. The horrible, intense pain that seemed completely insurmountable at the start really does ease. I didn't believe Howard Fillit's email when he sent it to me. Early on, it was all so completely incomprehensible. My mind wasn't functioning on all cylinders and I had no basis of comparison to anything else in my entire life.

But the reason I could not believe the pain would ever ease up was not just because it was unique. Logically, it was impossible to imagine it would just go away, since the source of the pain wasn't going to walk back through the front door to alleviate it. I just assumed this was my future and it would remain as such for the rest of my life.

It would not.

But the pain eases in its own course. It takes longer for some, shorter for others, and there is absolutely no predicting which it will be for you. Why did my friends Mike, Harvey, and Adam move into new relationships with seeming ease? We were all devoted husbands and happy in our marriages. Just plain luck meeting the right person early on? Was I too attached to Lisa? Was it self-pity? This remains a mystery to me.

After five years, I have found methods that help. Focusing on being grateful for what I had and have has eased the pain:

- A wonderful marriage with the right person who loved me as much as I loved her. Not everyone gets this.

- A wonderful, smart, funny, and beautiful daughter who has her mother's intelligence and wears her eyes. Lucky again.

- A fulfilling job with a wonderful boss to keep me busy with work I could focus on during this difficult time. Lucky still.

- My own good health. I hate to admit it, but I always took it for granted. I try not to anymore.

- Cancer can break a family financially. I was lucky to have a good insurance plan.

How horrible it would be to lose one's savings on top of everything else.

- And there are little things I do throughout the day that bring me joy: I look forward to that first cup of coffee in the morning; workouts in the gym; great music on Spotify; a brother-in-law, sister-in-law, and sister who are always there to take my calls; the same with friends.

- I don't have Lisa anymore, but I've developed substitutes, people I can share my thoughts with, people I can laugh with, people who remind me there are still folks in the world who care about me.

Now, if I constantly repeat all the above bullet points and keep repeating them, I will, hopefully, continue to believe them. Having said all this, some days are still hard and it's not always clear why.

A good therapist helps a lot, and I was very lucky to find a great one. I was not a believer in therapy before. I am now. Early on I was fortunate to find someone who fit, who is very smart and very caring. I wish I had done this 40 years earlier; it might have saved some really stupid mistakes on my part (that's for another, longer book).

It makes me sad to write this, but there is one more factor that may be the most important of all which has helped more than all the above: Lisa becomes more distant with each passing day. During our entire marriage, we never went longer than a few days without seeing each other, and that was rare. We spoke on the phone and texted each other all day long. We would talk for hours at night. When something bad happened, I called her first for comfort and when something good happened, I called her first because I knew she would get so excited. She did the same. Lisa was the greatest cheerleader I ever had in my life. She was the last person I saw before I closed my eyes and the first person I saw when I opened them.

When you don't see someone or talk to them or laugh about the day's events for weeks and then months and then years, it has to have an impact. How could it not? It's inevitable.

Time has left her behind. She never heard the word COVID, she doesn't know the results of the 2020 election, she doesn't know her daughter graduated from college, got a master's, and has been working now for two years. She doesn't know the struggles that I've had in her absence and the terrible sadness I've lived with for these past five years.

The number of big events to come will only increase that distance. Claire now brings friends home who never met Lisa. There will be that huge missing presence whenever Claire gets married. A new generation will arrive, and Lisa will be just a name to them, someone they never knew.

So, Lisa is no longer ever-present. The best way I can put it: she is distant, and she grows more distant, and that's OK. It seems natural. Even when I look at her picture, it's different, it's less immediate. She is no longer constantly on my mind.

In spite of this growing distance, I still believe that I will recognize her immediately when I see her again, and a big part of me believes that I will, somewhere down the line. But she doesn't dominate every thought the way she did in that first year...or even the first two years, and frankly, that's a relief.

I don't think I ever feared death. I think I will be surprised when it happens, if I am conscious of it, but I certainly never dwelt on it the way some people do. Now, I have no fear whatsoever because I believe in my bones that she'll be waiting for me. I will see her, and that belief sustains me, it gets me through the months and years and that has helped me move ahead.

Our conversation will continue. We will laugh together again. My arms will gather round her, and I will hold her again. We will pick up right where we left off, or at least I hope so.

And a new clock will start running.

CHAPTER 31

Standing on the Platform, Waving Goodbye

I REALIZE NOW, AFTER READING everything I've put down, that this is not just a book on bereavement. It's a love story as well.

Just as religion is intertwined with death, so is love.

In his review of Didion's book, author James Runcie, who is himself a widower, writes, "If love can knock us sideways when it arrives, then its old enemy, death, can do something equally powerful when it doesn't so much as turn up on the doorstep, but sits down opposite."[14]

Like Runcie, like Didion, like almost every human being since Genesis, I've been knocked sideways by both. In the process, I've experienced something equally powerful: redemption.

---

14   James Runcie, "Five Best Love Stories," *Wall Street Journal*,
        February 11–12, 2023.

It's just that it took the first two—love and death—to understand the third.

Let me explain.

I mentioned earlier that I managed to make a lot of wrong choices throughout my life. Some rather spectacular. Then one day, no different from any other, a friend asked me the world's most mundane question. What still amazes me is that something so incredibly humdrum would have such a powerful impact on the course of my life.

"Would you like to meet someone?"

It was as simple as that...the question that changed everything, the question that brought Lisa into my life: *Would I like to meet someone?* I even remember where I was standing in the subway station at 103rd and Broadway that morning when he asked me.

"Of course," I said, "sure." But even as the words came out of my mouth, my expectations were pretty low. *One more wasted evening*, I thought.

Why? Because in the past I had either been uninterested in almost everyone I met...or when there was the slightest spark, the other party had no interest. Everyone else around me seemed to figure out how to work this formula, but it remained a mystery to me.

As it turned out, Lisa later told me she wasn't terribly optimistic the night we first met. "I was thinking I was just coming there to meet someone," she said. "I never thought I would meet *you*."

I was even thinking of cancelling at the last minute because it had been a long day, the weather was lousy and, to be honest, I was so down about the entire process that there wasn't much reserve left. But since these friends lived around the corner and had gone to some bother making dinner, I felt obligated.

Let this be a lesson to everyone out there still in search of someone—don't lose hope and certainly don't say no to *any* possibility.

I arrived ahead of Lisa, so I was there when she walked in. The attraction—I'll even venture to say the *promise*—that this woman brought into the room was immediate. Throughout the evening, I tried to avoid staring at her eyes too long so she wouldn't notice. They were the most penetrating blue eyes I had ever seen. Her smile and her laughter warmed my heart.

There is one more critical part to that night that still mystifies me all these years later. It makes me think there was, indeed, more at play here…an upper hand, if you will.

The conversation was lively and wide-ranging throughout the dinner, until we realized it was well past 11 and a school night. Lisa and I finally stood up, thanked our hosts, put on our coats, and said goodnight.

Then, suddenly, we found ourselves standing in the hallway waiting for the elevator, staring at each other, without the other couple to back us up. I think we both became a little nervous.

To break this awkward silence, I turned to her and said, "Well, that went rather well…do you want to get married?"

She just stared at me, not knowing what to say. Long afterwards, she said she had thought I seemed "OK" until that moment. Then she thought I was nuts. When we got down to the street and she got into the cab, she said, "Goodnight," but what she really meant was "Goodbye," never expecting to see me again.

But over the next few days, when she repeated this exchange to friends, everyone laughed and said, "Maybe you should give this guy another chance." She explained that she had been on so many bad dates that she had clearly lost her sense of humor.

In telling this story over the years, I've said I was just trying to break the awkward silence in the hallway with some levity. But on further reflection, I had never said that to anyone four hours after meeting them.

Why would I have said something like that? What was it in that one dinner that prompted such a suggestive response, a response so unlike me?

Remembering my friend Rabbi Besser's thought about marriage, perhaps I finally, even sub-consciously, heard and this time actually *listened* to the heavenly announcement. Perhaps I finally grasped the equation that eluded me up until then. In more poetic terms, via F. Scott Fitzgerald, perhaps I was just waiting to hear "the tuning fork that had been struck upon a star."

Less than one year after that first introduction, we were husband and wife, and our daughter was on the way. Everything we both dreamed of came true.

So, as Runcie wrote, if that first act can knock us sideways, it stands to reason that the second act will do the same. But here's the difference between acts I and II—and it's immense.

We are not thinking of any possible end when we are experiencing life's penultimate moment. Falling in love defies every other chemical, physical, even nuclear reaction in the universe. It sets fire to every synapse in the body, it expands the mind like no drug could ever do, it causes our hearts to palpitate and, yes, it can even make us crazy. So of course, we expect something this powerful to last forever.

"In sickness and in health…'til death do us part?" Sure, we hear it, we even agree to it, but we really don't believe it at that glorious moment. It's *pro forma*, like the instruction manual that comes with the washing machine.

How could this dazzling moment *not* last forever?

Newton's third law states for every action (force) in nature there is an equal and opposite reaction. Well, there it is. When one party actually exits, it's got to hit you just as hard as when they arrived.

Now, here's the hopeful part of Newton's law: perhaps this particular bond that is more exquisite than anything else we will ever encounter continues even *after* the curtain falls on the first act.

How can I not be thankful for what came my way on that most random of nights?

So, with love and death and gratitude combined with the seemingly arbitrary nature of life, I leave you with one last story.

There is a small train station in the town of West Bend, Wisconsin, where the old Chicago and Northwestern line connected the small towns and farms north of Milwaukee to the outside world. The station was built in 1900 and serviced passengers until it stopped running in the late 1960s. Once abandoned, the station fell into disrepair for decades, but it was brought back to life and beautifully restored in the 1990s as the Washington & Ozaukee County Land Trust. Even the station master's office, with its polished dark wood cabinets and numerous drawers, looks just like it did when I was a child.

Often, the head of the Trust would see people old enough to have used the old station standing outside, revisiting their past experiences. There is something uniquely romantic about the old days of train travel, unlike planes and automobiles today.

One day, he noticed an elderly woman standing by herself for a long time, seemingly lost in her thoughts. After a while, he grew concerned and came out and asked if she had any questions, if he could help her?

"No," she told him with a warm smile, "thank you."

Her smile comforted him. He began to tell her about the restoration, when she interrupted him with something that took him aback.

"This was the last place I saw my husband," she said matter-of-factly.

At first, he didn't quite understand, but then she continued with something much more personal.

"We came here to the station with our young daughter to say goodbye when he went overseas during the war."

The Trust director was moved, but he wasn't completely surprised. He knew people had all sorts of memories, some so enormously happy and some heartbreakingly sad. The trains that came into this station picked up couples going off on their honeymoons. It took families to the great cities of Milwaukee, Chicago, and even New York. It also was the place where soldiers said goodbye to their families and where caskets were brought home for burial.

"You would think this station would be a sad place for me, but it's not," she continued. "I like to come here and remember him."

There have been times since Lisa died that I've thought about that station that I loved as a child. But now, in my new memory, passenger service on the Chicago and Northwestern never stopped. The huge, streamlined diesel pulls in with its brakes hissing, just like it did before. The station master still sits in his office checking his pocket watch. The calendar and schedules are posted on the wall of the waiting room out of a Rockwell painting. The train rolls in right on time, bringing with it all the joys and happiness of my childhood. There is the great cast of personalities I once knew that overpowers anything sad to come. Mrs. Wickesberg and all the other moms never left us. Just like the woman standing outside remembers her husband gone now for over half a century, I now have someone who rises above all the others and who never went away.

I hold on to my memories as tight as I can. Whether it's in a restaurant where we once sat, on a street where we walked, under the theater marquee where I waited for her before the show began, on the pier at the lake in the early morning where she drank coffee in a white porcelain mug, or near Claire's school on the East River, where we are rushing for the winter assembly—Lisa is with me again with her luminous smile, her penetrating blue eyes, her incredible warmth, and her overpowering love for me and for our daughter.

After five years without her, I am so grateful for these memories. I never expected to write these words at the end of this story, that I consider myself lucky, but I do now. Yes, there is still loneliness, there always will be, and it can still be a struggle to place gratitude before the loss.

But most days I am now winning this struggle.

I sincerely hope you will too.

POSTSCRIPT

Throughout it all, I knew how Lisa's loss affected me. I did not really know how it impacted Claire.

Even though we are talking about the same person, losing a spouse and losing a parent are not the same at all.

In the year after her mother's death, Claire put down these thoughts for a college writing class. I learned a great deal from this essay by Claire Rose Kozak.

When I Dream, It's Always Cold
By Claire Rose Kozak

In 2004, when I was six years old, my parents and I drove to Wisconsin. This wouldn't be something worth mentioning except this particular trip featured heavily in the stories my parents told over the years. We'd made the trip from New York City (home) to West Bend, Wisconsin (never quite home) before and we would make it again many times in the years to come. But this was the first and last time my parents made the mistake of driving.

I was strapped into my bulky, '90s-style car seat, goldfish shards and books digging into my skinny first-grade thighs. I waited as patiently as a six-year-old could for us to finish the traffic-plagued trip to LaGuardia Airport.

But the expected turn off the highway never came. I resisted saying something for an hour or two, hoping I'd miscalculated, before I leaned forward as much as my car seat would allow and asked my mother when we'd be getting to the airport. She shared a look with my father, and then laughed, as if in surprise. "Oh honey," she said, the smile on her face half-pity, half-apologetic, "we're driving to Wisconsin."

I'm told that in that moment, my six-year-old self clenched her little fists and said with the utmost gravity she could muster, "You made the wrong choice, Mommy. You made the wrong choice."

At six years old, I certainly didn't possess the vocabulary to express the breadth of betrayal I felt at this unprecedentedly stupid idea, but I'm fairly sure my feelings would have translated to you guys really screwed up.

My family spent most of our summers in Wisconsin. My father inherited the lake house from his late parents who inherited it from his grandparents...a patch of lakefront five minutes away from the sleepy little town of West Bend. The cottages didn't match the fancy country homes that many of my New York classmates had, but it was the lake itself that made the place worth loving.

The clear, frigid water was smoother than the finest linen, and I'd spend each day swimming until my fingers and palms pruned, seaweed stroking my legs like mermaid hands grasping at me from below. I'd pass hours on my back under the water, nose pinched tightly between my fingers, staring up at the sun through the surface. The lake was so still some days, so crystalline, that I could see the cloud formations above through a watery film.

My mother always made a big production of getting into the water. She was a slim, attractive woman, looking more like she was in her mid-thirties than her late-forties. Her appearance spoke of fastidious care—gorgeous haircuts, well-pressed clothes, well-fitted pantsuits that were covered with her pristine doctors' lab coat. At the lake, however, I saw the less polished version of my mother—gym clothes and ratty bathing suits, hair dried out by the briny lake-water. But she was still beautiful.

I know that every child thinks her mother the loveliest woman in the world (and her father the most handsome). But I never grew out of that notion, not with my mom. She was always the most beautiful, and bravest, and smartest. Her nails, unpainted, still complemented her long, graceful fingers. Her nose, although crooked, sat beneath eyes more piercingly blue than my own. Her entire body spoke of elegance, a kind of grace that I, a gangly child and later a self-conscious teen, could only hope to mimic.

But all that grace disappeared the moment she'd place one foot on the first rickety wooden step down into the water. She'd shriek, tensing up and arching her back like a displeased cat—and she wasn't overreacting. Wisconsin summer nights are nothing compared to Wisconsin winters, but they can still plunge to offensively low temperatures. The lake was never warmer than the coldest olympic pool. She'd yell and swear all the way in until her head was finally submerged, then swim along as if she'd never fussed at all.

When I was fifteen, my mom got sick.

She refused to swim in the lake, convinced that the seaweed, or something else in the water, would give her some terrible infection that her decimated immune system wouldn't be able to fight off. She was probably right, but I could tell she missed the water terribly. I would look up as I paddled by in a languid backstroke, sun warming my belly, to see her watching from the boathouse window. I could never make out her expression through the screen, but I could guess what she might be feeling. Or at least, I assumed I could, with all the confidence of a fifteen-year-old, of someone who knew nothing about grief or loss or how it felt to know that you were dying. She always denied that she missed the lake. Illness makes liars of us all.

Imagine my rage, watching her slip away from me even as I paddled out of view of the lake-house. Imagine my grief as I realized that one day, she wouldn't be waiting there with a towel to welcome me home when I finally returned, dripping lake-water across the creaky, hardwood floors.

My family spent most of our summers in Wisconsin until my mother's diagnosis. In the months before my freshman year of college, my father and I were marooned in Boston, passing time between a hotel room and the tiny chairs in the ICU. I spent my days watching IVs drain, drip by drip, and wondering how so many needles could fit into one small body. I'd never thought of my mother as small before that summer. But she looked like a child in that hospital bed, swimming in sheets, surrounded by wires and beeping machines.

That summer, I began suffering from reoccurring dreams. I say suffering because they haunt me to this day, more than three years later. Each night, I'd fall asleep in Boston to find myself in the lake at West Bend. I dreamed I was swimming there, the water like warm silk, sun far above the surface. When I finally needed to come up for air, I'd almost make it to the surface before I awoke, usually in a cold sweat, always in Boston, and never where I wanted to be. I dreamt of swimming until I left for college in late August, and dreamed of it again the following summer, when I returned home to New York to look after my mother again. During those humid summer days, I began to do the unthinkable—longing to be in Wisconsin, even if it meant driving. An interminable car ride of flat cornfields and glaring blacktop was worth it if it meant I could feel the lake water on my skin.

I never got my wish. I remained in New York that summer until I returned to college for my sophomore year, visiting the lake most nights, swimming in my dreams. I never resented my mother for marooning us in city after city. Instead, I resented Wisconsin, resented this place that called to me with a seaweed-filled-siren song. I hated the lake, hated the drive, hated how far I was from a place I never intended to love.

The last time we went to Wisconsin, we flew. This time, I was nineteen, a sophomore in college. This time, we went in the dead of winter. This time, I sat with my dad on the plane, and my mom travelled separately, below the cabin in the cargo hold with the luggage. This time, we were on our way to bury her. We went to Wisconsin this past January to lay her to rest in the graveyard where my dad's family has been buried since they came to this country more than a century ago. This time, the trip, although it took only two hours, and not two days, felt truly endless.

Standing in the cemetery, I felt that same blinding rage from that car ride all those years ago, that same conviction that someone had really screwed up. But who was to blame? My mother, for having the nerve to die on us? My father, for being the one who survived her, the one I was left with? The weather, as the mourners at the grave felt the warmth drain out of our toes and the -5° temperature and howling winds? God, for sending a blizzard, as if her death wasn't causing enough grief? Or me, for not being able to focus on the ritual, and thinking instead of silky water and warm sun and anything but the soft snowy hole in the ground before me, and the gaping hole between my ribs.

Since January, when I think of the lake, it's always winter there. Now when I dream, it's always cold.

My family has collapsed in upon itself, from a complete universe of three to an enormous, empty room of two. Incredible, how one person's absence can break apart what seemed so infallible, so permanent. But I guess that permanence was an illusion, as deceiving as the still water of the lake, or the silence of a snow-covered graveyard. As endless as a two-day drive, and as shockingly brief as a two-hour plane ride.

My family tells the story of when we drove to Wisconsin in the summer of 2004. When I say my family, I mean my mother. When I say tells, I mean told. When I say story, I mean an echo of a happier time—the echo of my mother's voice, the echo of her elegant hands on the steering wheel, the echo of her half-apologetic and beautiful smile.

My reoccurring dreams still haunt me, but it's always snowy now, suspended in perpetual winter like some twisted fairy-tale version of the place I loved. The lake is the bottom half of this distorted snow globe, distance folding in on itself to place the cemetery on the shore of the lake, one lone grave standing tall above the rest. Shake it, and you'll see snow swirl around the frigid mourners. Rattle the globe hard enough, and maybe the lake water will unfreeze and run cold and clear to flood the cemetery.

Maybe then, my mother can finally swim again.

Warren Kozak married Dr. Lisa Krenzel in 1998. They raised their daughter, Claire, in New York City and lived happily together until Lisa's death in 2018. Warren still lives in the same apartment and works as a writer. Claire lives nearby and is now a high school teacher.